In
Each
Moment

Also by Paul Lowe

The Experiment Is Over

Du Selbst Sein, German Edition

El Experimento Ha Terminado, Spanish Edition

Sound and Silence (compact disc)

In
Each
Moment

*a new way
to live*

Paul Lowe

Edited by Devon Ronner

LOOKING GLASS PRESS

Copyright © 1998 by Paul G. Lowe and Devon Ronner
Edited by Devon Ronner
Text Design by Devon Ronner
Photographs by Devesh Komaromi
Cover design by Ralph Dodd
Produced by Peanut Butter Publishing
Printed in Canada

c/o 212 Babbacombe Road
Torquay, Devon TQ1 31A
England

Canadian Cataloguing in Publication Data
Lowe, Paul G., 1933-
In each moment
ISBN 0-9684109-0-1
1. Self-realisation I. Ronner, Devon S. 1947-
II. Title.
BF637.S4L68 1998   158.1   C98-910799-X

LOOKING GLASS PRESS
Vancouver, British Columbia
Canada

For Elise and Walter Lowe,
with deepest love and appreciation.

In Each Moment

In Each Moment

Contents

I. In the Beginning Are the Words / 1

The opening chapter explores the unique meanings of key phrases and terms that Paul Lowe uses. The words expand and clarify each other and form a foundation for the ideas expressed throughout the book.

II. Uncovering the Love / 13

Love is not what we think it is. Love is completely beyond our understanding and yet it is the essential energy that vibrates in our being. As we live more truthfully, the veils we have constructed between ourselves and the experience of our loving essence fall away.

III. The Greatest Intimacy / 23

Our behaviours keep us separate from one another. We have developed these patterns in the hope they will help us feel safe and protected, yet they actually prevent us from feeling alive and connected to ourselves and others. There *is* another way we can be together.

IV. Here for the Adventure / 29

This chapter is an invitation to play with an idea that you may find yourself beginning to remember. We moved from oneness into duality in order to experience ourselves. Now the experiment is over and we can come home—to ourselves.

V. This Is It / 33

We have been told that there is a state of enlightenment we can reach. This is not true—there is no state to attain. Everything is already here, expressed in every moment. This is it. When we are totally here, in complete acceptance, the state we call awakening is realised.

VI. Freedom and Joy – Right Here, Right Now / 43

We are addicted to avoiding experiencing ourselves as we truly are. Working on ourselves to become a "better person" is one of the most common modern addictions. There is nothing wrong with any of us and the path to freedom is more available than we could ever imagine.

VII. Work – Is It Really Necessary? / 47

People tend to think about work in terms of survival. Yet life is not about struggling—life is an adventure. It is about the possibility of expanding consciousness in each moment. Life responds when we make ourselves available for delight and fun, and that includes what we usually call "work."

VIII. Relating – An Invitation to Expand / 55

The changes that have the potential to transform our lives have to do with our inner world, with consciousness. We are continuously being invited to become more conscious and to live on this planet without fear. Our relating with people provides many opportunities to explore this possibility.

IX. When the Spirit Takes Over / 65

Consider this possibility: Here on planet Earth we are participating in the experiment of adopting a physical form in order to experience reality. The game is to be in this form—with all its built-in programs and conditioning—and be free.

X. Far More Than A Machine / 73

Most of us believe that our bodies, minds and emotions *are* who we are. We have forgotten that we are far more than the machinery with which we have become identified. There is a part of us that is separate from our human equipment. It is called consciousness.

XI. The "I" Is Not You / 81

Most of the time we live at the level of our personality—identified with the "I"—separate from each other as well as from a connection to something beyond ourselves. We have the potential to drop down into an experience of the unformed where there is no separation.

Ava and Paul Lowe at Harbin Hot Springs, California,
September, 1997.

Foreword

Over the last twenty years that I have known Paul Lowe, I have appreciated his unique ability to be gentle, generous, yet also fierce and uncompromising. I have admired the way he has devoted himself to meditation, spiritual practice and study and to the karma yoga of selfless work.

Paul may be the most highly trained spiritual teacher in the western world. I believe that the counsel of one who has explored the far and near reaches of the human psyche so thoroughly, as well as travelled the world as extensively as he has, is most suited as a guide to those on the path of awakening.

Paul and Ava, who work together, inspire us to live at

our maximum potential every moment of every day. This potential is here, now, moment to moment. In fact, this moment is all there is. To live this way is a matter of choice, awareness and understanding of what I call the "Energy-Ecstasy Connection"—the ability to experience the union between life and spirit, or energy and consciousness.

I like to hear Paul and Ava present their way of remaining light, aware, loving and playful in all situations. It has been a great inspiration. I rejoice in the feeling that I have finally discovered this ability for myself. Read this book to find how, for yourself.

Margo Anand,
author of *The Art of Everyday Ecstasy*
and *The Art of Sexual Ecstasy*

About the Author

The facts about Paul Lowe are not really important. But what he has learned through his life experience—about waking up, about freedom, about a depth of aliveness in each moment—is important.

Ultimately this book is about love—a love that is impersonal and yet intimate with all of life. This is love as the author lives it—without judgment, without knowing. Safety, security and predictability have never been his priorities. He has made himself available to the adventure of living without conditions and demands on life. He has devoted his life to being conscious and fully present in each moment, as it is. He has a great deal to share.

He and his partner, Ava, are loving examples of the possibility of being together in harmony and joy—without compromise. They are married, but it is not a marriage as most know it. It is a union of moment-to-moment relating, with no conditions, nothing taken for granted and each completely available to respond appropriately to the invitation of every moment. Their relating is a vital expression of the love this book embraces. They travel around the world with a group of friends, inspiring people by their example and sharing with others the delight of living in the present.

Paul offers evening talks, weekend meetings and longer events where he assists people to the realisation of their maximum potential. He is also now devoting time to being with people who are experiencing or may be on the verge of experiencing what is called the state of "no-self." Wherever the next edge of life is, he goes there—and beyond.

Preface

Hello Dear Reader,

I have "found" a way of living where you can feel happy and joyful and free of fear. I would love for you to have the opportunity to experience this possibility, to see yourself and life more clearly and to recognise the areas in which your life is not working. Most of us just get through the best way that we can, hoping for as little trouble as possible rather than being open to happiness and realising that it is conceivable for everything in life to be wonderful.

If you read this book without agreeing or disagreeing, rather taking the suggestions and insights as hypotheses, you may come to see that there is much, much more to life and to yourself than you have imagined.

I used to have a sense that I was missing something, that there was more to life than I was experiencing, and that I was the only one not "getting it." Yet as I looked around, I began to see that no one appeared to have it. In fact, everyone I knew seemed unaware that there was more to life than they were living. They were concentrating on survival rather than attempting to discover what life is really about.

I looked for this missing aspect in all the "normal" spheres of life—in work, marriage, friendships—and never discovered it there. I found that nothing on the outside, in itself, would create a deep sense of fulfillment. I could have concluded at this point that there is no such thing as true happiness or real harmony, but an intuitive sense that there was much more to life persisted.

I began an exploration to see if there was, indeed, anything I was overlooking. My life became devoted to the possibility of expanding human consciousness. For many years I travelled around the world, experiencing everything I could. We might say it was a search, yet in another way, I was simply responding to life. I was living and enjoying each moment for the sake of itself, rather than working towards a goal of "awakening."

It wasn't that things did not get better; in fact, the more total I was in whatever I was doing, the more I did get out of *life. But I never felt that intangible, deep sense of fulfillment. I had spent years and years and tried everything, and still that state eluded me. After years of being total in everything I tried, I gave up; I really gave up.*

Then suddenly it happened. There was nothing dramatic, it just happened. And I cannot say what the "it" was. I cannot even say exactly when this awakening started because when it did, I realised that "it" had been there all the time. This place is with everyone, always. It is with you, the reader of this book. But because you are looking for what you think it should be, you do not recognise that it is already there.

What changed was my perspective, and with the change came a wonderful feeling of well-being and an indescribable freedom—freedom from stress, freedom from fear and the freedom from the illusion that there is somewhere to get to or that there are goals to attain. Yet, at the same time, I also saw that anything is possible—much more than we have ever imagined. We live just a fraction of our potential. We can go on expanding, and no matter how good it is, it can always become more wonderful.

All the ordinary elements of life have not stopped just because I have had a shift in perspective. In fact, they seem to get better and better.

Meeting my partner, Ava, and relating the way that we do, feels like another confirmation for me of how wonderful everything can be when we live truthfully, consciously and are present In Each Moment. Being together is as clean, honest and as open as it can possibly be—living life, living our truth, and sharing every single thing. There is no sense of separation and no secrets. To depths and depths—there are no secrets. We change and expand all the time, and in our individuality, we fit together. To us, living this way is simply a matter of intelligence.

We can share our experiences with you in the many events we offer at the evening talks, weekend meetings, two- and three-week gatherings. They are times of great fun, with people like you from all over the world, and you are welcome to join us, anywhere, anytime. But you do not need to wait for that. You can have it now. In Each Moment.

You already know what is written here. It is simply a matter of letting yourself remember. So, read without trying.

And have fun!

With love,
Paul Lowe

Suggestions for Reading This Book

This book consists of eighteen talks by Paul Lowe. The talks took place during meetings in Bali, Germany, Austria, Australia, Mexico, Canada, Italy, Chile and the United States, from 1995 through 1997. Each has been edited into a chapter.

What you are about to read is Paul Lowe's truth. It is the truth of an ordinary man who is travelling an extraordinary path—a path that is available to all of us. This volume is an invitation to approach what he offers as a hypothesis that can assist you in finding your own unique way of being. It is an invitation to experiment, to play with the possibility of opening to an entirely new adventure of life, to have fun and to come home to yourself.

Many of the talks are responses to questions and issues people have presented to Paul. Though we have chosen not to include the dialogue between Paul and those attending the talks, we wanted to preserve the feeling of immediacy and direct contact as much as possible. We have attempted this by retaining Paul's use of the pronoun "you" wherever it seemed appropriate. We invite you to consider yourself part of this intimate conversation.

You may feel drawn to reading the chapters at random, rather than the sequence in which they have been printed. A chapter title may attract you, or the book may simply open to a section on its own, like a casting of the I Ching. We encourage you to consider playing with the idea that whatever chapter chooses you may have meaning for you, in that moment, and to read with a light heart.

Paul's talks are threaded with references to teachers in both the eastern and western spiritual traditions. He also alludes to findings in psychology, science and medicine. You can find further details on many of these references in a chapter at the end of the book called References and Notes.

Paul has always said that what he offers has nothing to do with the words. The words are the carrier wave that conveys a vibration which resonates in you so that you may feel another level of yourself. As you experience the resonance, you begin to recognise that you already know what is being expressed. You begin to remember what has been within you all along but has been forgotten.

As you read the words in this book, I suggest you let go of straining for understanding. Let go of seeking meaning, answers, logic and consistency. Read with soft eyes. Let the feelings evoked in you be your guide. Allow yourself to be with the energy of the words, the images they arouse and the remembering they may stir in you.

If you go to your mind, if you try to understand, you will contract your life energy. Stay open, neither agreeing nor disagreeing with what is written here, and something will happen beyond thinking, beyond comprehension. Paul has often said that what he is attempting to share cannot be said. But it can be heard. So, listen. And enjoy yourself.

Devon Ronner
Bali, Indonesia
May 1998

Chapter I

In the Beginning Are the Words

One of the powerful aspects of language is its capacity to take familiar concepts and amplify them to encompass new dimensions. In his talks, Paul uses a number of words and expressions that may seem familiar, yet they convey fresh and unique ideas. In order to avoid misinterpretations it seemed wise to identify these phrases as early as possible and include the reader in a common understanding of their meaning.

With this in mind, Paul and the editor sat down with a tape recorder to discuss these terms. It quickly became apparent that what had been intended to be brief definitions blossomed into a much fuller explication of some of the key facets of Paul's perspective. Each phrase conveyed nuances that kept revealing layers of meaning as Paul reflected on the words. Ultimately, the phrases all weave together, clarifying and expanding each other. What was initially intended as footnote material has evolved into the first chapter of this book and provides a foundation for all subsequent chapters. The ideas expressed in the following pages emerged from those conversations with Paul.

Maximum Potential

I use the term "maximum potential" to express in a fresh way an indescribable state that we have endowed with many different names. Those people who have awakened and attempted to share the impossible nature of their experiences have interpreted the unexplainable through the filter of their own distinctive individuality. Heraclitus called it "the Hidden Harmony," Lao Tzu named it "the Tao," Jesus referred to it as "the kingdom of God" and "the peace that passeth all understanding." Currently, the word "enlightenment" is frequently being used. These are all phrases used to communicate something that cannot really be named.

When we use a word such as enlightenment, each person interprets it through the mind, which, of course, is the only way you can make an intellectual interpretation. Yet, in this case, we cannot really know the state this word is attempting to describe, for we cannot know it through the mind. This inexplicable experience occurs when the mind stops or is bypassed, therefore it is impossible for the intellect to comprehend it.

A spiritual seeker tends to understand enlightenment to be a pure state which excludes other states of being. When Buddha was describing the condition of being he had experienced, he did so by delineating all that it is not. And so it is with this state. It is not light, it is not dark. It is not here, it is not there. It is not you, it is not me. All these things that it is not. The seeker's mind then tends to think that enlightenment occurs when we do not have anything we may consider inappropriate—when there is not anger, greed or lust. That is a natural conclusion to draw, but it is not what is meant. In fact, it is not like that at all.

Of course, now you ask, "Then what is it like?" Therein lies the difficulty—explaining the incomprehensible. At the moment the term I am using for this state is "maximum potential"—it is not love and it is not hate *and* it is both. The mind does not know what to do with that. How can it be both? This is the dilemma science has faced since it discovered that light is both a particle and a wave at the same time. If it is two opposites simultaneously, what is it really? It is something that the mind cannot explain. And yet, it is.

To me, the experience of maximum potential means not excluding or rejecting anything *and* not identifying with anything. In this very moment, which is really all there is, maximum potential includes the state of the body, the action of the mind, the movement of the emotions. It includes judgment, not as a negative or positive attitude, but as the observations and conclusions you might make of the other. It includes your awareness of the environment, the sound of the bells in the distance, the wind in the trees, the rain on the roof.

It includes everything without focusing on any one thing specifically. Then the mind, attempting to understand and conclude what it should do with this information, might think, "Oh, this means when I hear the bells I mustn't focus on them." But it is not anything that is done with the mind. In this moment you expand and include everything. You include the function of the mind, but you do not focus there.

From the perspective of maximum potential, the question to ponder is, "What is the maximum potential of this moment, including the action of the mind, the state of the body, the movement of the emotions?"

To make it more practical, consider this example. When you are talking to someone to whom you are attracted, you include all the things associated with that circumstance. You include the fact of your attraction, the possibility that the person may not be available, your thoughts that they may not be attracted to you, the fact that you have a partner and how your partner might feel if you were attracted to someone else. You include all these things and as you expand to encompass everything, you would not decide to say something and you would not decide *not* to say something. You would not use your will to select a course of action, yet a response would come through you.

When you allow whatever wants to be said, *you* do not say something, something says you. Life will live through you when you include everything without rejecting or focusing on any single thing.

The essential self, the purity and limitless possibility contained within all of us, is surrounded by and encased in our conditioning, our unconscious beliefs about who we think we are and how the world functions. This conditioning leads us to believe ideas such as, "This is who I am. I am a person who can do this and can't do that. I am shaped by the facts of my past. I can change some things and some things I cannot change."

This way of thinking reflects the story we each have about ourselves and we take this story as a fact or immutable truth. But it is neither a fact nor true; it is simply a limiting perspective we have adopted about ourselves, assisted by what people have told us is and is not possible for us. When we are in our maximum potential, we accept these ideas, but we disconnect from them, and we are free to remind ourselves, "Anything is possible in this moment. I include my story; I include what I think are my restrictions. And I can disconnect from all of this. I am available for anything that wants to happen in this moment. Anything. I accept the fact that I think that this is not possible, and I do not identify with that thought. I make myself available to anything, including that which is beyond what I think is possible."

When you are ready to experiment with this approach, your whole life can change because anything really is possible. We are restricted by what we believe our restrictions to be, to a level that is unfathomable. We can move mountains. We are the creators.

Source

"Source" is unexplainable, yet it has been given many names. It has been called the Tao, the Hidden Harmony, "the peace that passeth all understanding," "the kingdom of God." This is the way my mind interprets it in order to share it. When we let go of all forms of identification with time and space, with knowing, with the need for safety, security and predictability, there is a disappearance, which means there is no identification with what we call the "self." Then there is no self as we know it and the mind cannot understand that. I call this state the unformed. The source is the unformed. It is not a white star and it is not a black hole. It is in perfect balance, in perfect neutrality, therefore there is no form. Then, from this state we create form according to our desires, although we usually do not recognise them as desires.

As I understand them, the aboriginal people of Australia are very close to this way of being. They say if we do not name a thing, it will disappear, so we have to sing its song in order to keep it here. The rock, the bird, the mountain, cannot exist without our naming it. Without our identifying it, everything will disappear back to its source, to the unformed. For us to keep anything here, we have to acknowledge it, appreciate it, name it and sing its song. We are not aware that we are doing this, but we are holding this reality as we know it by identifying it as such. If we did not do that, we would go to source, which is life in an unformed state.

Each person *is* that state of the unformed, not a part of that state. Many of the eastern philosophies express the idea that everything in existence is created from this unformed state, from the whole, and the whole remains intact and undiminished. Each person is not part of existence, each person *is* existence. The mind cannot understand this because it works in duality, but each part, each person, is the whole and is the source. The game in this dimension is to have a direct experience of source. Once this is realised, the struggle is over—nothing is ever serious again; life becomes fun, a series of events to experience and savour deeply. We are not here to understand or to control life, but to be present and enjoy the maximum potential of each moment, just as it is.

Choicelessness and Being Present

"Being present" is a state which includes everything and makes no choices. You include the condition of the body, the mind and the emotions, as well as the situation as you see it in the other person and the environment around you. You include all these things and if you remain open and do not identify with any part of it, then choices are made, not *by* you, but *through* you.

Let us consider a situation in which we usually think we have to choose something. Imagine you are offered two jobs and one seems to promise more money and prestige than the other. Normally you would go to the mind and take in all the considerations for both sides. But if you do not try to decide, if you do not contract and focus with the will on outcome and the future, if you simply stay there, a choice will come. Very often it may not seem to be a logical one. It might be the position with less money and the mind might call out, "But there's more money here, and prestige. Take this one."

When you go to "choicelessness," you move into a timeless state. In a way that is difficult to explain, you start to experience the future, although you are not aware of doing so. You include all the facts and something keeps saying, "Take the other one, take the other one." Usually you do not pay attention to that voice, but if you do listen to those instincts, you will find something is choosing you. What may be occurring is that some months in the future, the position that appears to be the better one may be involved in a takeover bid by another company and you would have lost your job if you had taken the "better" offer. You do not know that, but you are aware that you feel something that may be difficult to understand. Go with the feelings, the intuition, not with the mind. That is choicelessness.

All that I have expressed about choicelessness applies to presence as well. Presence is being in this moment with acceptance, including all the facts and disconnecting from them. And something then chooses you. You probably will not understand it. You may not feel safe or secure and little will seem predictable, but there is something there. Intuition, a gut feeling, is offering you information. This is the realm from which the great inventions are created, important business deals are made and the big breakthroughs in science, the arts and all aspects of life arise.

On every level—personal, professional, spiritual—this information comes from the feelings that emerge when we are present, not from the logic of the mind. The flow of life streams through us in moments of presence.

Inner Dialogue

Most people are not aware that they are thinking all the time, day and night, even when they are meditating and sleeping. I call this perpetual chatter of the mind the "inner dialogue." Most people are not in contact with this process; they do not realise that the mind is continually saying things like, "I like this, I don't like that. They like me, they don't like me. This feels safe, that feels threatening. . . ." This dialogue goes on incessantly, just below our awareness. One of the major keys to awakening is becoming aware of it.

Behind the inner dialogue is a matrix, a form, that says, "This is the way I want things to be." However, the way we want things to be often seems so impossible to us that we do not even recognise that we are wanting it. Of course, most people want to be rich, to be safe and secure; they want to be with a loving partner and have the best house, job and car. They want life to be the way they want it to be. But they eliminate it all and believe that with their circumstances, education, upbringing, it is not really possible for them. Yet the fact is, this hidden matrix drives our lives and creates resentment, because we deny ourselves the things we really want.

It is possible to have what you most long for if you are ready to acknowledge how you want things to be, accept it as a preference, but not as a rigid demand, and return to this moment, available to what is happening, right now. A preference says, "This is the way I would like things to be and if it is not this way, I will be in my maximum potential with the way it is." A choice demands, "If it is not the way I want it to be, I am contracted and resentful. I am against something or someone."

It is possible to set yourself free by recognising, in each moment, the whole process of the mind, acknowledging it and sharing what is appropriate. Disclosing your inner dialogue reveals your truth in each moment, most importantly to yourself. Generally people do not realise it is their truth. They deny it and this is the source of their misery.

This tendency to unconsciously overlook your inner dialogue is a huge barrier to your freedom. It is what you keep between you and yourself and between you and the rest of the world. It is so simple. You do not need to look at the things most people call "spiritual." You do not need to go seeking anything. If you would start to become aware of your inner dialogue and share it, you would transform yourself and you would transform each other. You would cut straight through the blanket in which you bury yourself from life—your own internal chatter—and you would start being here with yourself and with each other. That is when life really begins.

Chapter II

Uncovering the Love

When I look at people, I have the knack of seeing beyond the personal identities that most of you confuse for yourself. And all that I see is love. That is what I see and that is all I have to share. You are in pain and you do not need to suffer. You are in distress and there is no need for it, for you *are* love.

There is nothing you can do about love, because that is who you are, that is what you are made of and every cell in your body vibrates in love. You have forgotten this, but one day you will remember. When you remember, you will probably be slipping out of your body and thinking: "Oh well, missed again!" Yet it can be different for you.

The adventure available to us is to remember all this while you are here, in your bodies, and to allow yourself to have fun. It is time for you to cast off the struggle. The love is already in you; it always has been and always will be.

As you read this you might think you understand the words, but it is not really about the words. Love is something else entirely. Love is not what you think it is. Love cannot be thought, neither can it be felt. It is beyond anything that is comprehensible. It is "the peace that passeth all understanding." It is within you now, and you can realise this, wake up to this, dwell in this at any moment. The more vulnerable you are, the more willing to experience and share the depth of your feelings, the more truthful you are with yourself and each other, the closer you are to that state of love.

We keep ourselves from realising this indescribable place of love by our automatic behavioural patterns and unconscious reactions—by controlling, by keeping busy in "doing" so much, by manipulating to get our way—all the strategies we developed in order to survive as children. These patterns worked then, but now they are in the way of realising the depth of love within us.

Each one of you is a work of art that is covered and distorted by your conditioning. The essential self is inside us in its purity. However, most of you believe you are unworthy and you attempt to earn love by doing things. Then you tend to experiment with not doing those things to see if others will still love you. All of this is based in the belief that you are not lovable unless someone loves you. That is not true.

Whether or not people approve of you, or like you or express any of the responses we confuse with love, it has nothing to do with you. You *are* love. Until you truly experience this you will continue to compromise yourself for the approval of other people's neuroses. When someone says they love you, they usually mean, "My neurosis is comfortable with your behaviour." It has nothing to do with love, for love is unconditional and that kind of love is very rare.

Most of the time you are working to attain other people's approval, not love, and approval of your behaviour at that, not of your essential self. You will never find the love I am talking about on the outside, and it will not make any difference if you do something to get it or if you do nothing to get it. As long as you are striving for something from someone else, you are not seeing yourself clearly. You are as you are. When you are ready to be more present you will start to see the way you have covered up this essential self with fear, conditioning and unconscious behaviours. You can begin to let them go and allow the purity inside you to infuse your life.

In response to your conditioning and to your personal life experiences, you have acquired layers of protection over this essence of love. Now the invitation is to let all these layers drop away, to refrain from using your defences and to allow your vulnerability. As you become more vulnerable with each other and are more real and truthful, you will start to realise many other depths of yourself to which you have not felt connected.

I know it is possible for you all to set yourselves free at any moment, but it is difficult to explain how to do it. I can say the words, yet it is not really in the words. The important thing is this: You need to connect with the part of yourself that has not been loved, nourished, supported and appreciated. You need to allow yourself to be vulnerable and to feel.

Deep within you have been hurt, repeatedly, and now you are defended and suspicious, always trying to understand as a means to feeling safer. Your system is on alert, expecting the worst. Some people expect physical damage; others, mental or emotional pain. This has kept you locked up from yourself, others and your maximum potential. Rather than going to your defences, you need to open to the vulnerability that is deep inside and be there with your feelings, not avoiding them nor giving energy to them with your thoughts and fears. Simply be there, present and available to experience yourself in a way that will probably feel new and uncomfortable.

Most of us become self–conscious rather than be present. The mind clicks in and starts to think, even when we are alone, "What will they think about me? Am I doing it right?" You look at yourself through what you imagine other people are thinking about you, projecting your worst fears from the past onto them. In doing this, you hardly ever really see each other. When you come together you are so self–conscious, so self–centred, that you do not see the other.

Nor is it likely that you can see yourself clearly until you have reached a certain stage of consciousness. Until then, you look through the conditioning of the mind that someone else has given you. You see yourself through other people's distorted perspectives. Because of this, you have grown up believing that you are stupid, wrong and unlovable. You believe that your uniqueness, your way of seeing things, your way of living are bad because you are not the way someone else's neurosis wanted you to be—a way, in fact, those people could not themselves be. But they wanted you to be that way and so you have denied yourself and have developed certain behaviour that is not real for you.

It is very difficult for you to see this, because every time you look at yourself, you look through this old conditioning. Your conditioning is very strong and you have not been trained to be present, to expand your awareness to include your thoughts, physical sensations, feelings, the people and things around you. You have been trained to think about things and to believe that thinking is presence. Thinking is not presence—it is "not being here." Thinking is neither experiencing nor feeling. It is thinking "about."

You have not been present, therefore most of you do not realise what is really going on. You are being continuously affected by your conditioning, on a subconscious level. You are here with varying levels of awareness, but underneath there are fears and disturbances of which you are not normally aware.

It is possible to sit and start to become aware of much more. It is not easy but it is possible. It requires being present, moment to moment, noticing how you are being affected by your conditioning and, if possible, being with friends who keep reminding you that you have lapsed into the old, unconscious behaviour; reminding you that your smile is not real, that you are getting angry rather than feeling your pain; reminding you that your face is blank and you are not showing your feelings; reminding you that you are going over the top of yourself with your energy or disappearing inside. You need the support of having these things pointed out as lovingly and nonjudgmentally as possible, because whatever you are doing is not wrong or bad, it is just keeping you from yourself.

I have a conditioned pattern that still occurs with me, though it has become much less powerful. When I enter a room to talk with people, I am expecting them not to like me. This arises from thirty years of my telling people what they have not wanted to hear and experiencing the reactions they tend to have. Of course, the reality is people respond with a great deal of love and gratitude for what I am offering, and there are also people who are very angry with me. This system is always anticipating trouble and if I am not conscious of this expectation, it affects my energy. I have to be aware all the time: What is the truth? What is really going on?

You all have hundreds of programs such as this operating. If you are not with them and present, they affect your energy. When I emphasize how important it is for you to be present, I know that you may think that it sounds so simple it cannot possibly make much of a difference. But it makes an enormous difference. It can change your life.

The encouragement is for us to be more present, more aware of what is going on, all the time. The difficulty is this: The mind functions on the premise that it has to think about things and so the mind is identifying and naming everything continuously, registering whether it is safe or threatened. The mind does not see reality, it sees its concept of reality. It sees everything in terms of good and bad, right and wrong, appropriate and inappropriate that it has learned from someone else. It labels everything according to other people's ideas.

That is really what the mind is: a program full of someone else's ideas based on the past. In our natural state the mind does not judge, because the mind is lean and clear and carries only neutral information, such as what name you are calling yourself, your address, the practical things needing your attention. That is the function of the mind in its natural state, but its natural function has been distorted and it has developed in such a way that it continually judges. The mind is busy naming things.

Jesus spoke about the possibility of being beyond this state of mind. He said: "When you see the inside as the outside, the outside as the inside, the up as the down, and the down as the up . . . when you see a man as a woman and a woman as a man . . . when thine eye be single . . . then will you enter into the kingdom."

When the dichotomy of the mind is allowed to disappear, then you will see directly. At the moment when you look, the mind classifies this as "man," then this man reminds you of your favourite uncle and you feel guilty because you have not answered his last letter . . . and it continues. You are not seeing the person. The mind is playing the game of naming and taking you out of the moment.

When you finally do wake up and see, you really are not seeing at all. You simply *are*. In that moment there is no separation between the seer and the seen—there is only one. From the oneness comes a concentration of energy, a more compacted energy, a form, a gender, a uniqueness. But because you have been brought up with so much fear, the mind is always working, splitting things up, categorising in its attempt to protect itself.

Your system—the mind, the body and the emotions—has been damaged by your conditioning. It is not irreparable and it is damaged. The pressures you live with have put your system out of balance. There has been so much fear and you have worked hard to cover up the fear. You put up your chin, you half smile and say, "Everything is all right. Everything is just fine." You have been saying that to other people and to yourself for a very long time. Now you can start to let go. The way you are living is not all right. Deep down, very little has truly felt fine. All that can change now. It is time to move closer to your truth and to feel more deeply. It is time to return to your essence of love.

Ava and Paul Lowe
Summer, 1996

Chapter III
The Greatest Intimacy

When we meet each other we usually *do* something rather than simply allow a true meeting. But unless we are very present, very aware, we do not notice what we are doing. Often when we meet, our energy shifts down into survival mode and our behaviour moves into unconscious patterns. Yet, most of the time we do not recognise that we are making these shifts. We have done this so often in our lives that it has become automatic.

The shift to survival is rooted in our experience as children. At that time we were not used to being in the world and we tried to avoid doing anything wrong or getting into trouble with the adults upon whom we were dependent.

We did this in an attempt to invite the love and connection we felt we needed to survive at that time. As children, it was rare that anyone truly saw us, met us, connected with us and appreciated us, and so we developed behaviours to avoid the pain.

Now as adults, whenever we meet others we automatically go on alert, into our conditioning and those learned behaviours. We go further away from our source, our vulnerability, our deep self–acceptance. We rise up out of our essence into a form of self–protection. Each of us has developed a different pattern of defence for survival. Some of us have become automatically aggressive, some passive; some of us inflate our behaviour and feelings and go over the top of our true selves, some make ourselves very much smaller than we really are; some pretend we know everything, some nothing at all—and everything in between. It is very rare that we are here—simply here—with ourselves and each other, feeling just who we are in this moment, in the presence of another person.

When we revert to these automatic patterns we prevent ourselves from moving to deeper levels of feeling. We rise up into behaviour rather than dropping into being, dropping ever closer to source, to "the peace that passeth all understanding." Our behaviour is not who we are, it is what we have created to protect our vulnerability. Yet we have forgotten this and for the most part, we have become so identified with our behaviours that we have mistaken them for ourselves.

It *is* possible to disconnect from automatic patterns and drop into a deeper sense of ourselves that feels vulnerable, sensitive and unknowing. This part is not self–centred; it is not focused on the self in a contracted, judgmental way. It is expanded and full of acceptance, allowing ourselves to be who we are, as we are. From this vulnerable place, our awareness includes the other person but is not focused on them. We do not modify our behaviour to fit this other person. Rather we include them in our consciousness and allow modification to happen on its own. As this person comes into our awareness, our energy field adjusts without our having to do anything. When we are present in the moment, change happens on its own.

We have been afraid to be with ourselves in this way because as we drop deep within, we lose touch with the familiar. We lose our identity, our sense of who we are and who we are not. As we let go of the safety and security of thinking we know, we drop into the vastness of the unformed, of source.

We are on the cusp of a new dimension, a new vibration of being, of consciousness. In order to be available to this new level we have to adjust. We do not have to do this adjustment through the mind; in fact, we cannot. We do it by being present unconditionally and allowing the adjustment to take place on its own. To be present in each moment we need to slow down—to slow down our physical movements, to slow down our mental activity and to become more aware of the emotional shifts happening inside of us.

We have a possibility now to disconnect from the past. The past is doomed to repeat itself because it is only capable of projecting itself onto an old, familiar future. All thought is based on the past and can only restrict future possibility. We can be present, now, in each moment.

Each of us is like a chrysalis and we are emerging as butterflies. We have been used to being caterpillars and we have been used to being wrapped up and contracted. Now we are coming into a new sense of our own beauty and it feels strange—even though it is so beautiful. We are used to being bound up and restricted, so the freedom seems frightening at first. These wings, this new sensitivity, this new level of freedom seem so unknown.

We need to adjust and the adjustment comes through being present, by allowing what is. If you feel your old fear, feel it fully—do not do anything about it; do not cover it up, do not energise it. If you are looking into someone's eyes and you do not know what to do or say—do not do anything, do not say anything. Drop inside and feel yourself, deeper and deeper. Even someone you have known for years and years is new in this moment and so are you. Be with this moment and you will feel another depth, another level of sensitivity. All this brings with it a feeling of vulnerability. Allow the vulnerability, allow the not knowing —here, now, not knowing, being. The greatest intimacy lies in not knowing.

Stay open to your possibilities—they are vaster than you have ever imagined. Invite yourself, without pressure, to another level of aliveness, of presence in each moment and to another level of having fun. With yourself. With others. With all of existence.

"There are no rules for living because you are
unique. Find your truth in each moment and
dare to live it. That is the way to freedom."

Chapter IV

Here for the Adventure

Suggestion to the reader: The experience of this chapter can be deepened if it is read to you while you close your eyes. Another option is to record it and then listen to your own voice inviting you to consider this possibility.

In the beginning was the unnamable—let us call it "the source." And that is not exactly true, as there is no time in the dimension of the source—no past, no future. The source is one and cannot experience itself in its oneness. In order to have an experience of knowing itself, it split up into billions of parts, lowering its vibration to manifest at the material level. Each part appears to be separate, yet is still the source, whole and complete in itself. The source remains whole and intact. The split is an illusion.

Part of the illusion is the split into human form, into what you recognise as "you." You came here to experience duality—which has been termed "right and wrong," "good and bad," "man and woman," "you and me," "up and down." It is duality, not reality.

You willed yourself to forget that you are source in order to be complete in this experience. The experiment is over now. Whenever you are ready to disconnect yourself from duality, you can go home. You can return to the experience of yourself as source. You can disidentify from the vehicle you have come to call "myself." You are not your body, you are not your mind, you are not your emotions. You have them, they do not have you.

The vehicle you are inhabiting is programmed. *You* are not. That system has been conditioned. *You* have not. *You* are not the mind, *you* are not the body, *you* are not the emotions. *You* have thoughts, thoughts do not have you. Disconnect from them and you will realise your true self. *You* are the source.

Whenever there is a disturbing thought, you can disconnect from it. It is only a thought. You can disconnect from the "I," the personality, the character, the ego, the neuroses. As you disconnect from everything you think you are, you will find that something remains. "Thou art That."

The pleasure you feel has to do with the body; the happiness you feel has to do with the mind; the joy has to do with your emotions. They are dependent on the outside. They come and they go. Beyond that, is bliss. It is eternal, it is not dependent upon outside circumstances.

Allow yourself to disconnect from identification with the outside. Allow all of that to be there on its own—the physical pain and pleasure in the body, the misery and excitement in the mind, the disturbances and happiness in the emotions. They are not you. You are the one who knows that those things are there. You can watch them and take no notice, for "This too shall pass." Disconnect and you can feel the hum, the Om, the basic vibration of the universe.

Be fully in the moment, but not of it. Be total, but not caught in your totality. Be complete, but not holding, not identifying with anything. Allow life to live you. Let it come and let it go. Let it be there. Let it leave.

If the system wants to cry—let it cry. There is no need to get involved. That is not you. If it wants to laugh, let it laugh. That is not you. You are so much more than those experiences. "Thou art That. The Kingdom of God, the Tao, the Hidden Harmony, the Way."

Feel yourself expanding to include the sounds around you. Stop holding, and expansion will happen. As you stop identifying with the finite, the infinite is there. Allow expansion to occur, yet no one is expanding. Keep disconnecting from what you think is the source, the "I," or the personality. As you keep disconnecting, expansion happens. You are the falling water, the bird in flight, the wind in the trees. You are everything.

In a few moments, you are going to gently come back to the perspective that you have identified with—that which you call "I." You have chosen this form instead of being the bird, or the tree, or the wind, or the person next to you. Instead of being the universal consciousness—without form, without a body—you have chosen to experience the universe from this perspective for a while.

We know what one year is, what ten years are. We have a feeling for one hundred years. A thousand years are hard to grasp. A million years are impossible to contemplate. And life, scientists say, has been here for billions and billions of years. We are in this form for a very short time.

We have come here for the adventure. We are here for the experience—to taste, to feel, to laugh, to touch, to be touched. We are here to find out what it is like to split into misery and happiness. Now the experiment is over. We can start to come back into the one. As we connect with source, we do not have to take duality so seriously. *Now we can have fun.*

Chapter V
This Is It

For thousands of years there have always been a few
people who have sensed that there is something more to
themselves and life than was commonly known. Through
either design or accident, a number of these people have
had an awakening to something beyond their everyday
experience. No one has ever fully described the sensation of
that awakening. Jesus called it, "the peace that passeth all
understanding," which means that it cannot be understood.
Lao Tzu named it the Tao, the Way, and Heraclitus called it
the Hidden Harmony.

When everything else drops away from us, something
remains that cannot be described. In parts of the East, they

do not even try to explain what it is, they simply call it "The Fourth," while others claim something occurs when the seventh or crown chakra opens. There are many attempts to account for this inexplicable phenomenon—the realisation of the perfection of everything and every moment. The source, God, radiant darkness, the still point, however we name it, that place is within you now. It is you who is not being with that place.

The people who have realised this state have endeavoured to share it and inform us of the possibility that there is something beyond that which we call our normal experience. I say it is beyond normal experience because it is not an experience. Experience has to do with the senses, the senses have to do with the mind and the mind cannot comprehend, hold or expand sufficiently to include this. When you do not go through the restrictions of the mind, through the labyrinth of thought, suddenly something happens. This state is what is left when you disconnect from the mind—the direct experience.

Those who have realised this state have attempted to invite us to that place, but we do not know what it is. When we think we know, the thought is the barrier to the realisation of it, for if it is thought, it is not that. Those who claim to know are not aware that they do not really know, because it is not a knowing. It is an emptiness of knowing.

Many different methods have been developed to assist people to leave aside the self as we know ourselves to be, in order to have this experience of awakening. Yet the people who want most to go beyond the self are those who are very strongly invested in the self. It is the self that wants to go beyond the mind. It is the ego that wants to be without an ego.

The state we are talking about is selfless—there is no self. You, as you know yourself, however, will never encounter this state, because the "you" that you identify with is the barrier to this state. There is no such thing as self–realisation. The key realisation is that there is no self as we see it. The mind can only register phenomena in terms of time and space and separation, and this state is beyond the mind. As science identifies light as being both a wave and a particle simultaneously, so in this state everything is there and not there. It is not you and yet it is not, not you.

Different people have developed various techniques to help others awaken, and none of them really work. No technique works. The methods that may come closest to being effective are ones that encourage you to stay with the impossible—as in some types of Zen. During those times you may be asking yourself an unanswerable question, a koan, with such intensity and totality, that eventually the mind, just for a moment, gives up. That is the satori—the glimpse, the direct experience.

The methods that have been developed to attain this state are expressions of the developer rather than approaches that lead to a profound and enduring shift in consciousness. Ceremonies, clothes, sounds, temples and rituals have evolved and have nothing to do with awakening. At one time, the method may have been associated with a genuine experience of awakening, but followers have tended to become lost in the method rather than moving beyond it to their own direct experience.

People who have had the direct experience have left many clues about how to make ourselves available to this state. Usually others have taken their words, reinterpreted them to fit their own beliefs, frozen them in institutionalised practices and these have led us further away.

The saying, "Seek ye first the Kingdom of God and all else will be added unto you," attributed to Jesus, says, "*Seek the Kingdom of God*"; it does not say, "When you have attained the Kingdom of God, all will be added unto you." It says that with the very seeking, all else will come to you— meaning that life will start to work. You will begin to vibrate at a different frequency when your priority becomes consciousness—when you look for the maximum potential of each moment.

Buddha urged us to carry no food, only one robe, and never to stay in one house for more than three consecutive nights. In other words, life will take care of you; if you allow it, you will always get what you need. Live moment to moment, choicelessly, without exerting your will, and life will unfold.

Our conditioning has told us that there is a state to reach and this is not true. There is no state to attain. Everything is already here, expressed in every moment. There is no state of enlightenment. There are realisations and they continue to forever expand, as does the universe. We go nowhere until we are here. This is it. When we are totally here, in complete acceptance, the state we call awakening is realised.

The place in you that seeks this state of "enlightenment" does not know anything—it only thinks it does. When it decides upon a goal in the future, it chooses from the neurosis of this moment. When you open to the state of no–mind there is no future and there are no choices. This is it. From this moment of acceptance evolves the next moment, exactly suited to your maximum potential. It is never a coincidence, for wherever you are, you are where you are meant to be—where your maximum potential is unfolding in this moment. The more totally you are in this moment, the more beautiful will be the next one. Fight this

moment, and you will have to fight the next one—
even harder.

If you are looking for this state, you will not find it.
Do not bother to knock, you do not really know how or
where to request entry and there is no place to enter. Stay
present and not knowing and allow the illusion that you
do know or that you need to know, to fall away. In this
very moment is the experience of freedom. It is you who
is not with the experience—not that freedom is separate
from you. The Kingdom of God is within. Buddha said:
"From the whole came the whole and the whole remained."
From the One, from the unformed, came the parts, and
the whole was unaffected by the release of the parts because
each part is the whole. Thou art That. It is a conundrum,
a puzzle, a game, an invitation, a challenge, a mystery
never to be solved.

You have to want whatever you call this state
totally and do absolutely nothing about it. Be in the moment
and keep disconnecting from the mind and the will that
say do this or do that. Open your senses and expand.
Include as much as possible and whatever is appropriate
will become clear for you in that moment—where to be,
what and whom to be with, what to do. You will never
need to go to the mind to make another decision again.
When you are in the stream of life, you *are* life. There is no

separation and there is no such a thing as choice. It is all happening, now. This is it.

Here is a perspective to play with that can support an expansion into life: "This is who I am right now. I am grateful for everything. I am joyful for this very moment and everything that I have encountered and felt. All that I have done and that has been done to me is included in my huge volume of experience and I am floating on this sea of experience. If there is something else, I am available to it. I will be here totally and unconditionally for anything that comes and I will feel whether this is appropriate for me. If it is, then yes! If it is not, then yes, it is not. Never no."

Sometimes we may confuse this state with the sense that nothing is happening, so why bother, and we let ourselves slip into lassitude. Although in this state of allowing we are not doing anything or going anywhere, it is totally alive; it is throbbing and tingling in each moment. The past is finished, it is over, so we disconnect from it. We have received what we needed and it has brought us to this moment. We do not need to use the past as a reference point to the future. It is just a basis of experience and here we are, now, ready to respond to whatever comes, in whatever way, but never because we are going to attain something. For there is nothing to attain.

So, if you are drawn to a teacher, you go, but you do not

go to them to get what they can give you. You go for the plane journey, for the taxi ride, for booking into the hotel, for sitting down with this person. You go to be with them, not for what you are going to attain, but for the experience of each moment. If you have gone to get something, you are dead on the way, and by the time you arrive there, you will be even more dead and harder to wake up. This moment—this is it! This is your master. This very moment is your teacher. The air, the subtle sounds around you, the heat, the presence of other people, they are all here to assist you to another depth of living. If you are drawn to be with somebody or something, let it be for the experience, not the outcome, for there is no outcome. There is only now.

When you truly realise this and you accept it, you soar. If you realise it and resist it, it is awful, because there is nothing else, there is no point to anything, there is no reason for living, there is nowhere to go and nothing to do. Nothing out there "works." Look one second into the future and there is just desolation. Be unconditional in this moment and you are in the unexplainable state of bliss. Resist in the slightest way, and you are in hell. In each moment be open, be a yes to what is possible, and suddenly, you are with another level of yourself, another level of life, another wondrous adventure. It is all in each moment, now—not what may come later.

And what happens when all this is accepted? What is

this unexplainable state? Everything and nothing. It is not happiness, not joy; it is not bliss, not pleasure; it is nothing you can describe and it is beyond anything you can imagine. It is not even beyond. It simply and totally, is.

You can say yes or no to this moment. If you say no, and it is something you need to experience, it will come back again and again. The Hindus say it can take 80,000 lives to experience it fully, unless you are ready to say, "Yes, this is it." Then you move beyond, except there really is no beyond and there is no movement. This is it. Right here, right now.

"When you feel in great distress,
do not pray to be over it.
Allow yourself to be with it.
This is acceptance."

Chapter VI
Freedom and Joy – Right Here, Right Now

There is a state of being that has been described as "the peace that passeth all understanding," the Tao, the Hidden Harmony. Closer to our own experience we tend to describe it as happiness, spirit, freedom, source or inner peace. Yet no word or phrase can really express the nature of this state.

This indescribable state exists equally in everyone. It has been covered up by what we have been told is and is not possible. From this conditioning, we have created patterns of behaviour that have literally buried our essence, our joy and our spirit.

We have assumed that there is something wrong with us and we have spent our lives attempting to put it right.

In fact, there is nothing wrong; all we need do is become aware, in each moment, of the behavioural patterns with which we have covered our essential self. When we are present to each moment we are on the path to "the indescribable," to freedom.

Much of the time we feel uncomfortable and we try to escape from this experience. We escape into our addictions, into alcohol, smoking, eating, anger, relationship conflicts or complaining. Working on ourselves can also be like a drug; it is what we do instead of being who we are, feeling what we feel. We can encourage ourselves to be who we truly are, to feel whatever we are feeling. There is no need to understand, nor to work on ourselves. All that is needed is simply to be ourselves.

When we do this, layers that cover what is essential in us then drop away on their own. Our system is self–healing if we allow it to be.

We have forgotten, or lost touch with knowing, that we are spirit contained in body, mind and emotions—and not a body that possibly contains the essence of pure spirit. This is the realisation that awaits us as we bring ourselves present to each moment. Everyone is looking for the way home. It is closer than we ever imagined.

A life of freedom begins when we realise deep within ourselves that we are whole and complete just as we are.

There is nothing to do, to find, to see, to understand, to work on. There is no right way to be.

Most people live on a surface level. When you live this way it is like being on top of a rough ocean, getting tossed and churned around with the waves of life. Peace and fulfillment come from living in the depths of ourselves, sensitively, with awareness, in each moment.

*"Being totally present in each moment
takes you beyond what you think is possible."*

Chapter VII

Work – Is It Really Necessary?

When people ask me about the meaning of work, I ask myself, "At what level am I going to reply to this question?" The way most people think about "work" arises from their conditioning and that is usually based on a level of basic survival. I am not really interested in that level any longer. No attempts to understand or change anything at this level will ever succeed in a deep and enduring way. It is now time to shift from survival to fulfillment.

In every dimension of life, we are always creating our own reality and that reality is totally mutable. Until now, most of us have created a reality fraught with struggle and distress. It is possible to create a life of freedom and joy.

In the Bible, Jesus is quoted as saying, "Take no thought of the morrow, let the morrow take thought of itself," and, "Consider the lilies of the fields, they toil not neither do they sow, yet Solomon, in all his glory, is not arrayed like one of these." Most of us do not live by such ideas of ease and fullness.

People tend to feel they have to struggle in life and work is frequently where the struggle is greatest. If people do not have difficulty, they often do not experience a sense of self because they define themselves through struggle. In adversity they feel themselves pitted against something or someone. Without that sense of "againstness," people often have no other reference point from which to recognise themselves.

Although they usually are not aware of it, people want trouble. They want conflict. They want to fight because that is how they give meaning to life. Without the fight, without the struggle, they do not have a sense of who they are. What they *could* have is a sense of something far greater and more wonderful. They could live in freedom and joy. This possibility is neither recognised nor supported due to our conditioning.

Our conditioning stems from someone or something— religion, government, parents—trying to control us. In order to control us, an attempt is made to make us feel uncomfortable. We are given programming that is unnatural to us about sex, food, work and having fun. All these restrictions exist in contradiction to who we really are and how we feel.

To find our freedom we have to move away from this conditioning and discover our truth for ourselves. At first that may feel very uncomfortable and unfamiliar. For instance, it is rare to find someone with a great deal of money and no need to work who can really accept their situation. Most people tend to feel guilty, to believe they are supposed to suffer and should work.

New Age thinking can be as destructive as the conditioning of the past. It is saying similar things—that we still have something to do, but now it is enlightenment that we are working towards. This is not true. There is nothing to work on, now or in the future. All we have is this moment—unconditionally.

Many people assume that work gives their lives meaning. As I understand it, there is no meaning as we know it. Life is about living. Life is about expanding our consciousness and maturing through experience. There is no particular direction to this, because each of us is totally different, unique. Each of us has our own way, but for everyone it entails allowing ourselves to respond to each moment, *unconditionally*. "Take no thought of the morrow."

Respond now. Be here, in each moment, letting everything go—all the conditioning and suffering. Dare to live in each moment, for the sake of that moment.

People often ask, "Don't we have to do something, do work, to survive?" There is no point in addressing this question, because from the mind's perspective there is no solution, no "happy" answer. We may say that we have to do something to survive, but everyone who has found freedom has said the opposite. They all tell us to live now, for now. We create our reality, so if we think we have to work, then we have to work. If we challenge existence and say, "Okay, take care of me," that does not work either. When we start to live our lives consciously, honestly and responsibly our lives will unfold in each moment. We will be taken care of and will never have to work in the way that we have known it.

The word "work" has the connotation of doing something we really do not want to do. That is not living. That is literally killing ourselves. There is another way. My two daughters are an example of this. They did not go to school until they were sixteen and within two years they had everything they needed, without being damaged by years of what we call education. One went on to university, and within another three years, had completed a degree and ranked in the top of her class. Both devoted themselves to their projects totally and joyfully. They were doing what they wanted, what felt connected with their hearts.

Life is not the way we think or have been told it is. If we listen to and come from our heart, we can have our heart's desire. My daughters were not acting out of survival. They were not listening to their minds, they were following their hearts. Hearts work, minds don't.

Life responds to us when we are available for delight and fun. When we focus on survival and struggle, that is what we get, that is what existence reflects back to us. If we *demand* fun, we are more apt to create resentment. But when we make consciousness a priority and are open for what is appropriate in our lives, we have fun and receive what we need. As the Bible reminds us, "When you become as a little child . . . ." As we allow our innocence, playfulness, presence to emerge—living the moment for the moment—then *life* happens magically.

Take a moment to consider this for yourself: When you are ready to let go of the old ways, the old beliefs and conditioning and at least take this new way as a hypothesis, you make yourself available to a totally different level of life. Then experiment—look at your life in every aspect, and move more slowly. Look at what is actually happening in this moment, not how you would like it to be, nor how you might pretend it could be. Ask yourself, "Is this my truth?"

Until you are ready to discover what your truth is in each moment and live it, your life will not flourish.

To make the new way practical, you really have to take time to be with yourself. Most people are dashing around trying to make things happen and they do not even know why they are doing this. You have to pause to look at your life, directly through your own eyes, not through someone else's technique or ideas of what your life should look like. Ask yourself, "What am I doing and what am I doing it for?" This is not the esoteric, "Who am I?" It is a more practical, "Who am I in this moment? What is life about *for me right now?*"

There are many depths of truth to explore. What is your truth about your relationship? What is your truth about your job, your fears, your longings? It is important to remember that the responses to these questions emerge out of the moment, and are not fixed, unchanging "truths." Often when you register your truth deeply, you mature into a new level of being and your truth in the very next moment may be different.

You have to stop running. You do not know what you are running from or where you are running to. Start being *here*, in each moment. If you do not like the job you currently have, what job would you like? What do you want to do? What is your heart's desire? When your heart answers this, your mind might say you cannot make money this way, but unless you acknowledge what your truth is, in this moment, you are running away from yourself.

When you recognise what you would like to do in this moment, you might find you need some credentials or training. Then the mind might come in and say, "You don't have the funds for that," or, "You're too old, too stupid to do that." Put aside the mind and what people tell you is practical and realistic. Make yourself available to what you want and be open to the possibility of support to help you realise it, then see what happens. You may be amazed by what occurs. Go for what you really want. Dare to go for your joy.

Another aspect of your conditioning is the focus you put on the end result, believing that *then*, when that occurs, whatever that result may be, everything will be fine. Life is not like that. Life is in each moment. It is about going for what you want *now*, not doing something in the hope that it will bring you what you want later. Your life is not working if you go to university to obtain a degree in order to get the job you want, but you are not enjoying the process of study. *Life is about now* and if it is not working now, it never will work. Out of this moment comes the next moment. And the next.

Most of us want what we want, not what we need. We are looking for safety and security, which exist only in our longing, not in reality. Life is here now and this now is totally unknown. We pretend to ourselves that we do know because we are terrified not to know, and then we forget we have made it all up. We want a house, a family, a job and we believe that once we have all that, everything will be all right. But it is not all right. Take a look around at yourself and the people in your life and you can see that that approach is definitely not working.

The myth we have been living is, "I've just got to get it right on the outside, then everything will be fine." But it is not about anything on the outside or arriving somewhere. It is about the journey. Everything is in movement and flux. Everything is changing. That is the nature of life. Until we are ready to be with change, we will always be fighting against what is. Life starts now and it can surpass whatever we may have imagined. Anything is possible.

Chapter VIII

Relating – An Invitation to Expand

One of the most significant changes that is happening on the planet is difficult to talk about because the mind does not want to hear it. We have been conditioned to believe that events on the outside control how we feel on the inside, which is not true. The changes that have the potential to transform our lives have to do with our inner world, with consciousness, not our attempts to change and control the people and things around us.

Let me give you a practical example of how this works. If someone you are attracted to tells you, "I would like to spend time with you," you feel good. The mind associates the cause with the effect. It reasons that this person wants to be with me, I get a wonderful feeling, therefore I feel good *because* they want to be with me. Someone else may say they do not like you, they do not want to be with you, and you feel unhappy. You associate this event with the feeling of distress, yet the event itself has no inherent power to affect you one way or the other. However, your conditioning on this has been so pervasive that most of your life revolves around the belief that you are controlled by external events. We have been brought up to believe in the principle of victimization. There is no such thing.

If we consider certain life experiences, we can see the fallacy in this way of thinking. Sometimes there is a potentially tragic incident in a person's life, yet there is an unexpected response to it. Someone sees a car accident about to happen to them and they are powerless to do anything about it. Suddenly, in the midst of it all, they have a feeling of euphoria, a tremendous sense of well–being. They watch the car coming towards them as if time has slowed down, and they have many crystal–clear thoughts. Or a totally opposite situation may occur—a person wins the lottery and when they are told the news, they have a heart attack and may die.

Here is how this process occurs. When something pleasant happens and you feel good, it is not the circumstances that make you feel that way. When the event takes place you say "yes"—you expand and make yourself available to what is. The acceptance and the expansion produce the good feelings. When something unpleasant or unexpected happens, you say no to what is happening, and that contraction, not the incident itself, produces the bad feeling. It is never the event, but how you are with the event that creates your experience.

If you are about to have a car accident, there is nothing you can do about it. If you say yes, you probably will not be badly hurt, because when you say yes, everything relaxes, the body flops around. When you say no, you become rigid and when you hit something, you are likely to break.

There are reports of people jumping from airplanes who found their parachutes did not open, and yet they lived. As one man recently recounted, he said to himself in such a situation: "My parachute is not opening; I am probably about to die, so I am going to enjoy this time of falling. . . ." He hit the ground, bounced and lived. There are many examples of people living through impossible circumstances because they accepted those situations and said "Yes!" You could say that the secret of life is "Yes!"

There is a secondary stage to this process. Take a moment to imagine this. Your beloved is spending time with someone else. If there is a total "yes" to this, you will feel no discomfort; in fact, you will feel a type of elation.

But if you miss that moment of yes, you might contract. Yet, if you accept the contraction, you will also feel good. If you fight the contraction you will surely feel worse.

All of this has to do with consciousness, not with particular incidents, and consciousness is the direction to which many of you are beginning to turn and explore.

As you are reading this, you have an experience of yourself existing on the physical level in the room where you are. Simultaneously you exist on other levels of consciousness, whether or not you have awareness of them. On the level where you usually live, you are asleep to the magnitude of your possibilities. Other levels within offer encouragement to open to experiences that will help you refine whatever conscious state you are in. These levels encourage whatever movement is appropriate to purify or to release what is often called Karma or the sins of the fathers.

You are continuously being invited to become more conscious and to live on this planet without the fear that normally rules you. One area that offers infinite opportunities for expansion of consciousness is in our intimate relationships.

Generally we attribute our discomfort in relationships to the other person. We believe we feel uncomfortable because our partner did or did not do something. That is not so; if you do not feel comfortable it is because you are not being responsible. You have probably been trying to make somebody else responsible for making your life work. That is not possible, yet it is what most people are doing. We are motivated to come together because we feel incomplete; we feel empty because we are not being ourselves, so we look for someone else to fill the gap. Then we cling to each other. But we have no control over the other person; they could leave at any time, and then we will be back with ourselves as we really are.

It will never work to look to someone else for your own happiness. No one else's life is going to make your life work. Like everyone, you are totally alone and you always will be. In that aloneness it is possible to dance joyfully with someone else, but most likely, you do not even know who you are, let alone someone else. You do not know how to connect with your own essence, so how can you dance freely with another's?

Your conditioning supports the jealousy and possessiveness that flow from the expectation that someone else can make you happy. If you do not face your jealousy you will be unhappy forever. Even if things are perfect, the mind will be saying, "What if . . . ? What if they meet someone they like better, who is richer, more beautiful? What if they discover how inadequate I am, how afraid I really feel?" And when you are not feeling good about yourself, the jealous feelings lie there, providing a justification for your discomfort.

The pain, anger and resentment you feel have nothing to do with the other person. It is your anger and your suffering, and if you do not face it with this person, it will be stimulated again, another time, by someone else. And if not by a person, it will be provoked by the unavailability of a parking space or by a computer that keeps crashing. The anger and resentment are in us and usually we do not take responsibility for them. We have been supported to be that way and it does not work. There is no such thing as a victim.

If your partner leaves you, you have participated in designing that—you chose that person, you are aware of what that person is capable of. Yet, nothing is wrong or a problem. Everything that happens is an invitation to you to let go of your holding, your resentment, your judgments, your determination to have things your way. You will keep giving yourself the experiences you need in order to realise a greater sense of inner freedom. If you are still fighting with the partner you now have, it would be fruitless to move, because you will only find another partner to fight with. It might take a year or two to warm up to the same place, but eventually you will again be fighting because the fight is in you. You are not being conscious about yourself. We choose the partners we need in order to help us become aware of the parts of ourselves we do not see or accept.

One day you will wake up from your conditioned reactions. You will find that when your partner is doing something that once distressed you, you will no longer be against them. You will feel something for them, as you recognise the pain and longing underlying their behaviour, but *you* will not be distressed or contracted. You will stay expanded. Then you can move in whatever way is appropriate. Being together has done the job; this partner has helped bring you to a place where you see yourself and them with acceptance.

As long as you believe your happiness is controlled by someone or something outside of yourself, you will never feel free. There are six billion other people on this planet that you will have to control; there will always be unpredictable weather, cars and appliances that break down, income taxes, car alarms that go all night. . . . There will always be something that upsets you, forever. This dimension is designed that way.

Until one day you get it—it just goes click and you are free. You realise your misery has to do with you, not the outside. Your resistance to the situation creates your discomfort. If you still have resentment, it's because you want it. When you are ready to let it go and start to live your life responsibly in each moment, everything changes. You live at a new depth of yourself.

When you disconnect from blame and resentment, there is a flow to life that I cannot explain. The "peace that passeth all understanding," the Tao, the Hidden Harmony, the Kingdom of God—we give it all these different names, and still it is indescribable. You have not been supported to relax into this possibility. You have been conditioned to survive, to struggle, to hold on even after the situation has ceased serving you. If you will start to live your truth in each moment, sharing your inner dialogue, you will find existence brings you exactly what you need. Whatever it is, do not hold it, just be with it. Then, when it is done, just float on. What you need next will come and find you.

There is a saying in the East that states when you take one step toward God, God takes ninety–nine towards you. When you start to live your life more consciously and honestly, many incredible things happen. Fully invite them, but do not get involved in them. You have an experience because it is what you need. Have it, but do not hold it, and be available for the next moment, the next experience. And remember, don't take anything too seriously.

As a support in releasing whatever anger or resentment you may have with someone that you are ready to let fall away, consider this gentle, active meditation:

Are you carrying any anger or resentment; are you blaming someone for your pain? If you are, take a look at letting it go. It is almost certain that the pain is hurting you more than them. Let your side of it go. Feel your heart. Take a few minutes. As you look, you might find an intense feeling inside because in that incident you felt pain. You felt your aloneness, your unworthiness, your indignation. Your pride was hurt deeply. You did not feel seen or loved or cared for. But instead of fully experiencing all those feelings, you reacted. You blamed the other person. Take a look at letting it all go now. Experiment with not holding on to it any longer and see how you feel.

Eventually you will come to see that everything in your life has been perfect—exactly what you needed at the time. It has helped you to grow and move and expand. One stage you may move through is forgiveness. Another stage is gratefulness. Especially consider this with your family. No matter how your parents have been with you, not only forgive them, but be grateful for what was there. Recognise their pain as well as your own. And then, let it all go. That does not mean that if they are unpleasant people you have to spend time with them. This is not about doing anything, it is about letting go of the anger and the resentment. Consider writing them a letter expressing the things about which you are grateful. Somewhere inside ourselves we are all looking to let go, to finish with the unpleasant past. Then we can start again. Right now, you can start your life anew.

Ava and Paul Lowe
Summer, 1997

Chapter IX
When the Spirit Takes Over

Suggestion to the reader: The experience of this chapter can be deepened if you have it read to you while you close your eyes. Another possibility is to record it and then listen to your own voice taking you on this journey.

I invite you to join me in exploring the possibilities suggested in this reverie.

Imagine that we are all together in a dimension that has no form. It is not material, it is pure spirit. There is no separation as we know it. We all can move in and out of each other. Then we hear about a dimension that has form, and something called "experience," which we do not have in this unformed state. This dimension, we are told, is created of material, tangible substance. We are intrigued and become interested in experimenting with this thing called "form."

We are told that before we can enter the dimension called planet Earth we have to adopt a form that will enable us to touch things and be touched. We will still be free spirits but we will be contained in a structure. This structure consists of a body that can have sensations in the mind, in the emotions and at the physical level. We will not easily be able to drift out of this body and then back in. In this new dimension we will become attached to the form and the game will be finding a way to detach ourselves, in order to be free, while continuing to exist in this form.

Imagine that you decide you would like to participate in this experiment. From this formless state you choose to take form and begin an experiment on planet Earth. There are no brand–new forms on this planet. They are all second–hand, all used, recycled. When you take a form, it already has built–in programs. These programs have been inherited from parents, society and thousands of years of conditioning. You are going to enter a machine, a very wondrous, very complicated machine that is also rather crude.

The mind in this machine is untamed—wild. It has a

will and thinks thoughts on its own. Emotions can be disturbed at any time. Before you enter this machine, you recognise that it already has a life all of its own, but it is mechanical, repetitive and addicted. It is addicted in that it has to have certain things or it feels uncomfortable. All of this occurs independent of you.

Once you decide that you want to experiment, you must adopt a machine to inhabit. Each of the machines is unique; no two are identical. Something that upsets one machine does not necessarily upset another one. When you enter the machine, you are stuck there until you find your way out. You find the path out by becoming one with the machine without becoming lost in it.

As you enter the machine you forget who you are, that you are pure spirit. Yet it is possible to become conscious of the automatic parts of the machine and as you do, you move towards remembering who you really are, you move towards your freedom. As you become aware of what makes it angry you get free from the anger. As you become aware of what makes it sad, you become free from the sadness.

Eventually you will be totally free within the machine; then it will start to balance itself. You and the machine will become one and you will be free to be here or to leave. It is a great and dangerous adventure, because you can get stuck in these machines for thousands of years. The machine dies, but it recreates itself and you are still caught in it.

In the spirit of this game, let us imagine that you have said "Yes!" and you are getting ready to choose a machine. When you enter this form, you will take over the misery and you will take over the joy. When you inhabit the machine you will also have a thing called sex, either a male sex or a female sex, or, if you are lucky, both.

Imagine you choose the body you are now in. You have chosen to be male or you have chosen to be female. You have chosen the shape, the look, the health and everything else. As spirit, you enter the body and you become who you call "you." Feel yourself coming into the body. It is not you. You are the spirit and you have adopted a machine— a body. The machine behaves automatically and you are going to take over the machine. You are taking over, not with the will, not by forcing it, but by becoming aware of this machine. Awareness will show you what makes it feel good, what makes it feel bad, where it is stuck, what its patterns and habits are.

As you settle into this form you will probably find that this machine has a mind and it never stops. It thinks all the time. Without you doing the thinking, it keeps thinking on its own. It also has feelings and sensations in the body all on its own, that have nothing whatsoever to do with you.

All you have to do is to be aware of being in there. It is a new adventure, an experiment. You are going to find out all about this machine: what it likes, what it does not like; what excites it, what makes it afraid; what it wants to do and what it does not want to do; to whom it gets drawn and from whom it moves away. You are going to experiment with this machine, but remember this: you are not going to take it personally, because it is not you. It is a machine that you are borrowing in order to have experiences in this dimension.

Now, spend a few minutes getting used to this machine. What is it like to be in it? How does it sit, what are the thoughts that are going on without you asking it to think? What are its feelings? Although nothing may be happening in this moment to stimulate it, how is it feeling?

You may notice that this machine can hear things; it picks up sounds outside of itself. It might have some pain or discomfort in the body. But remember, you are a visitor, you are simply noticing all this and watching the activity of the mind. What is this mind thinking? Is it thinking about what it calls the past? Strange, because that has nothing to do with you, you are just visiting. Then it starts to think of the future. Very strange, because that is not your future, that is just the machine thinking. You are here, now. You are watching. You are involved, in a way. You can have a good time, but it is not you. *You are the spirit within the machine.*

Slowly, as you become aware of the patterns of the machine, it will start to change form. It will start to match you. As you bring awareness to its actions, it will purify and become more beautiful and younger. You will become the source of this machine, its spirit.

As you continue to explore the machine you are in, you need to keep remembering you are in something that reacts on its own. It will be happy and unhappy without you having anything to do with it. Remember, you are the spirit in the machine—you are always watching. It might become attracted to someone, and that might be fun or it might be frightening. What is fun, what is being frightened? You do not know, you are here to discover all that. You are here to have these experiences. You are going to learn everything you can about the machine you are sitting in. Everything.

Now spend a few moments feeling yourself in the machine and experiment with moving some of its parts. You can move everything: its fingers, hands, feet. Sometimes it moves on its own. That is what happens when you are not conscious—it will act automatically. Remember, it will think on its own unless you are there, unless you are aware. The machine has a life of its own. It is up to you to be conscious and present and not let it live you.

You create your machine from the state of your

consciousness within the machine. You can transform this piece of human equipment, but you cannot do it with the will. The will is the part that is sick; it is the part that says no, that wants its own way, that creates what you might call the ugliness of the machine.

If you reject your machine, it will get worse. If you love it, if you care for it, if you see that it is not at its maximum potential and you devote your consciousness to being with it—it will transform. Eventually, it will assume an appropriate form that reflects the state of your spirit.

This is what I am encouraging you to do: Start seeing the difference between the automatic conditioning and the spirit in the machine. You are here to experiment. You are here to have fun. You are here to use your consciousness to set the machine free from the limitations of its conditioning. You have the possibility to be less automatic and more present, not by pushing, not by forcing, but by being very aware.

This machine has gotten itself into trouble because it is so strongly conditioned. Your spirit, your consciousness, can release it. The fears you have about any part of your body, any sensation, any emotion, are all conditioned—it has nothing to do with you. You can set your machine free by being present with your consciousness.

Think of it this way: You are in a machine that has been

mistreated. You need to love it and care for it and through this attention, it will find its freedom.

The game is to be in the machine and feel free. In order for that to happen, you have to feel the restrictions consciously. Experience them, be with them and then you can start to discover what these restrictions are. You could become contracted from something as benign as the sound of a bird singing, because, perhaps as a child when you did something others considered wrong, you were punished, put into your room alone, and a bird sang outside your window. Your mind might now associate a bird singing with punishment. It can be that trivial or absurd. The colour somebody wears or a particular tone of voice might stimulate unconscious associations and your body will react. You have to be there to discover what this reaction is, and to be with it. Eventually you and the machine will become one because you have become so free. Then the machine starts to respond to the spirit.

This is an imagining—and it is also real. You have lost touch with this reality. You have forgotten that you are the spirit in the machine. You are spirit that has taken on a human form, not a human with the possibility of realising spirit. You can start to remember who you really are, right now. You can start to come home.

Chapter X
Far More Than A Machine

Most of us spend our entire lives believing that our bodies, our minds and our emotions form who we are. We have forgotten that we are far more than the automatic machinery with which we have become identified. There is a part of us that is separate from the human machine. It is consciousness.

When we are not present with our consciousness, the part of us that is a machine goes on automatic pilot and runs itself. This is necessary in order to operate the essential life functions such as heartbeat, breathing, digestion, circulation, but for the rest of our being, the challenge is to be so conscious in each moment that we can take over from the machine.

If we are not present, the machine, directed by our conditioning, will assume control. This programming operates at a very low level of vibration, that of survival, and tends to be violent. It may manifest as the violence of thought, but nonetheless, it is violence.

When someone around you is unpleasant, you quickly revert to an automatic pattern and you have a reaction from the survival level. The challenge is to be there, available to override this instantaneous conditioning. When you are present, listening to what the person is saying and aware of the effects it may have on your body, mind and emotions, you will come to realise that the one reacting is not you. You are the one who is aware of the effect and therefore, you do not have to react nor suppress anything. You simply stand there, saying to yourself, "This person has said something that I find unpleasant to hear. My system is in a panic; it is uncomfortable and it does not want to be uncomfortable, so instead it is becoming angry or shutting off. I am not going to support that reaction. I am going to be here. I am ready to experience this discomfort and not escape into the addictive patterns of anger or withdrawal."

With that quality of consciousness you start to cut the roots of your conditioning and eventually, they will fade away on their own. But if you are not there and someone says something disturbing, the machine will take over, your addictive behaviour will be activated, and from then on you will be acting on automatic pilot. You will have to wait for the chemicals in your system to run their course, and then you can start again.

When a situation arises and you are not 100 percent present, you will react mechanically, like a computer that has been programmed from the past. Whether you react with a yes or a no, this reaction is not originating in the purity of you. It comes from the part that is a robot. When you are present and unconditional with whatever the maximum potential of this moment may be, all the internal and external influences will be there, but they will have no real effect on you.

If you associate with a "no" or a "yes," you are not aligned with your highest potential. There is something else watching, separate from your conditioning, that recognises the conditioned response and is closer to your source. If, at the moment you become aware of holding onto a "no" or a "yes," you let go of all choice, whatever is your maximum potential will happen on its own. If you attempt to stay safe, secure or predictable, you will use your mind to manipulate the moment.

It seems that it is a radical thought for many of us to

allow ourselves simply to experience our feelings, without denying them or inflating them. A question people often ask me regarding feelings is what they should do when they are feeling bad. The answer is, nothing. This is it. Of course you do not want to feel bad, but if you do anything about it, including using any techniques to clear it, it is your neurosis that is choosing, your neurosis that wants to do something to escape from the discomfort of the moment. Your system knows how to take care of itself. It knows how to heal itself; it is your mind that will not let it be.

When you allow yourself to be with the discomfort, you will feel what you need to experience. If you totally accept it, it will disappear. Resist and you are in misery. Accept and you are free. There is nothing you can do; in fact, all doing will only compound the situation. If you use a technique or take a drug, it will only be an anaesthetic to briefly numb the discomfort, and while you are taking it, the energy of the feeling is still building up inside you, waiting to surface again, probably with greater intensity.

You are going to have to deal with everything one day; you can either deal with it throughout 80,000 lives, as the Hindus believe, or in one second. If you have lost the moment by contracting or going unconscious, accept that you have lost it and you will find it again.

All of the experiences we have created for ourselves have

a vibration in our system in the form of cellular memory. Everything is in there. Not only our personal experiences, but the experiences of the entire universe are also vibrating within us and we each relate to the impact of those vibrations differently. Some people may have been sexually molested as children and are free from it, it is no longer an issue with them, so they do not think about it. Others may still be affected by these experiences, either consciously or unconsciously. There is nothing we can do about those situations from the past. If we are present unconditionally in each moment, all those influences will be there, but they will not affect us. The moment we go into thought, attempt a technique, avoid the feelings in any way, or we "work" on it, we are back in the mechanical level again and everything will affect us.

When we stop avoiding and accept our experience, the sensations will be in the body, the mind, and the emotions, but they will not be in the place that we will come to know as ourselves. We *are* beyond those things, yet we cannot make ourselves "go" beyond them. Include the mind, the emotions and the body with acceptance and you are here *and* beyond them. We cannot "work them through" because the one that is trying to work on them is the one that is neurotic and limited. That part of you does not see what is really appropriate; it only wants what it wants, not what it needs.

In fact, there is nothing that needs to be "worked through." This Is It.

You have been conditioned from the moment of your conception by things about which you have no idea—there are billions of influences. You will never be free of these and even if you could free yourself in this lifetime, what if there were a previous life and another one before that? The "work" would never end.

There is another way—disconnect from it all. You can allow the reactions, the feelings and the past to be there, yet you do not need to identify with any of it. None of it is you. When you are ready to be in this moment, unconditionally, your cells will shake themselves like a dog shaking off water, and they will shake off all the conditioning. Your cells will vibrate differently, but then the past will be gone, and the past is you. You will be gone and there will be no one you can call "you." You are the drop disappearing back into the ocean. You are the ocean.

Most of us want our conditioning because it gives us a sense of self, and the sense of self holds the promise of safety, security and predictability even though there are no such states in this dimension. The moment you do not want your conditioning, it is gone. It cannot stay in place without you. It is a rechargeable battery and it cannot hold the charge without you recharging it. Your life is exactly the way you want it in this moment and as soon as you want it to be different, it will change—instantly. You do not realise that you are perpetuating your life as it has been, that you are creating your reality out of your unconsciousness. Until you wake up to this, you will never feel free.

When we are ready to live our lives truthfully and responsibly, we will move beyond survival and awaken to another depth of life. The question to ask is not how do we get there, because we are already there, but rather, what is in the way? Greed is in the way; the need to feel special is in the way; our behaviours, the clichés we speak, the tone of our voice, the unaware smiles or scowls, the unconscious body postures are all in the way. None of it is wrong or bad, it is simply in the way of who we really are.

When enough of us are fully here to step each step, smell each smell, be in each look, touch what we touch, hear what we hear, for its own sake, in each moment, we will awaken to a greater depth of ourselves.

The time of individual awakening is over and it is now time for us to move collectively. Individually it is virtually impossible to awaken and continue to live in that state—not totally impossible, but virtually. It will happen as we create communities together that have gone beyond a certain level of self. And it is beginning to happen.

We are moving toward the possibility of awakening

collectively when we are here for ourselves through each other; when there is an intent to joyfully and playfully be more aware and responsible together; when, if someone seems to have gone unconscious or dropped out of the moment, someone else will be there to gently remind them. Eventually we will find the turnover point where we become more conscious than unconscious and as soon as we are over that 50 percent line something in us can open. Then we will live together sharing, being responsible and present so totally and unconditionally, that we will create a new way of living.

When we want this enough, when it is our priority, without being serious or complaining about it, our intention will activate a new state of consciousness, here in this dimension. It will also generate a force that will assist people who want to live in that way. It takes wanting it with every cell, throbbing with it . . . and doing nothing, going nowhere, not even meditating to attain it, but being so present that we are ready to respond to each moment, whatever it is, exactly as it is. Then we are there.

Chapter XI
The "I" Is Not You

There is a place inside of all of us which is empty and at the same time, full. It has no form, yet it is overflowing with energy. It is still, yet it is continuously moving, though this movement has no pattern. It simply is. Nothing goes on there, and yet everything is there, formlessly. Although this state is unnamable, we will call it "the source."

As with most people, you probably live unaware of this source in your daily lives. You live in your "I," which is full of mind activity that constantly measures and evaluates. It says, "I like this, I don't like that; I agree with this, I disagree with that; I think this is right, I think that is wrong."

Your sense of yourself revolves around that "I" to such an extent that you believe it *is* you. Yet that "I" is your ignorance. It may be how you relate to yourself, but it is *not* you.

When you are identified with that "I" you are in misery. The misery continues as long as this identification goes on. When you acknowledge it and then drop below that familiar sense of yourself into the unformed, you enter a realm where there is no "I," where there is no separation.

Most of the time you live at the level of your personality. This is where your opinions come from and where the need to see yourself as important originates. Even when you think of yourself as unimportant, you are still caught in the web of significance. To the universe, this significance means nothing. You are like an ant in the Sahara Desert talking to a grain of sand, saying "I don't like you" and fiercely believing it matters. You will continue to be lost in the fiction of your self–importance until you are ready to let go of that isolated "I," until you are ready to drop back into the ocean and become the ocean.

There is, however, no way of *you* going to the ocean. There is no way down; no matter what you do, *you* cannot go there. It is the separate "I" that wants to attain union and this is where spiritual seekers tend to become stuck. They feel the longing to melt into the sense of oneness, but the

"I" cannot go there. The "I" has to disappear in order to experience this state of the unformed, or source.

What you know of life comes through this narrow, tiny "I." We are told that we operate at 5 percent of our potential, and that small percentage is the "I." Science maintains we experience only one billionth of reality and this is squeezed through that "I," through the restriction of saying, "this is good, that is bad; this is benefit, that is harm." This is how we block the gate to the state that no one has ever been able to describe—the Tao, the Hidden Harmony, the Kingdom of God.

This indescribable state is here now, equally in everyone. It is the source. The more you try to search for it, the further you go away from it. Do not go seeking it; do not go demanding it. Simply allow yourself to be available to what is happening right now and it will find you.

Making yourself available means you include the mind that thinks, that wants to get somewhere, that complains, but you give it no energy, you do not reinforce it. If the body is uncomfortable, you acknowledge the discomfort and do what you need to do to adjust that, but do not make it your focus and do not make it important.

You all have this space inside, and yet that is not strictly true. You do not have it, it has *you*. The space is. It is your source. It is the unformed. Until you either experience this place, recognise it or take it as a hypothesis, you are in turmoil.

The turmoil you live in is generated by the mind. The mind is the part that determines what is good and bad, what is right or wrong. It is possible to hear how close or how far away a person is from the source as you listen to them speak. If a person is complaining or judging, then they are a long way from source. If their energy is neutral, they are less far away, but still distant from source. If a person is grateful, they are much closer. When your priority is placed on awareness, on being present in each moment with acceptance, you make yourself available to the experience of source.

Your complaints are all on the surface of life. When you identify with problems—having a relationship, not having a relationship, money, work issues—you are not going to be happy. Even when you do feel happy, it usually does not last very long. When you are ready to drop to source, an experience even more expanded than "happy" is available. The source is the one that is being aware of what is happening on the surface—but is not being the surface.

When most people start to seek they often suffer from the spiritual disease of "I–ness." It seems to be a necessary step for many. In one way, when you start to look for your maximum potential, or whatever you prefer to call it, you have to be selfish. You have to follow life for yourself rather than according to what others have told you. On the other hand, if you become self–centred, you become totally stuck.

Recently a man was telling me, "I don't enjoy riding my bicycle on the beach very much." He has contracted down to that tiny point where there is too much "I" and not enough beach or bicycle, not enough sky and wind. He needs to consider asking the bicycle if it is having fun today and if the sand is enjoying him being there. In so many ways we need to open up our world. When we get too focused on the "I," even when it is sincere, our life energy gets jammed up.

It is not wrong or bad to centre on the "I," but it is not being present and it will only lead you to misery and self–consciousness. Everything has a consciousness and when you become too focused on yourself, you get out of balance with the rest of the universe. Some people can be talking about themselves in the midst of a magnificent sunset, and they don't see it. We need to expand to include the "I" and everything else as well.

When we were born, we were all connected to source and we gave it up in order to know ourselves as separate. That was the experiment and now the experiment is over. There is a possibility available to us to return to source. When we do, there will be another level of consciousness, another level of vibration; there will be the experience of awareness and presence. We gave up our direct experience of source in order to return to it and be there with consciousness.

I am not saying that you necessarily know how to do this. I am just presenting you with the next possibility—the possibility of staying in the emptiness. Emptiness is not what many people think it is; it is not being spaced out. In fact, it is not really empty, it is absolutely full and totally unformed. It is the source of everything. When you go to speak from this space, it comes as a response, and the emptiness takes a temporary form as a word, action, thought or feeling. It does its job, and then drops back into emptiness again. You do not use your will, you do not actually *do* it. It does it through you.

It is all a matter of *being present in each moment.* Presence expands you. Being present is not thinking, yet it includes thinking; it is not feeling, yet it includes feeling. It includes, it widens out, it holds all sounds, thoughts, feelings and sensations. Yet it is not any one of them. It includes everything.

There is a knack to being choiceless and to being available to the flow of life without going to the mind to make decisions. Until you acquire it, simply be aware of the choice you are wanting to make. If you do not feel good, be aware that you would prefer it to be different from the way it is, but encourage yourself not to make it a choice, not to be attached to having it the way you demand. Leave space to let go of the tendency to say "no" to what is and allow yourself not to contract with the surface of things. Drop down again into the state of not knowing, into the unformed.

At your essence you are God. You are the "is–ness." I was going to say you are valuable to the universe, but you cannot be valuable to the universe because you are the universe.

"Acceptance and awareness
are the keys to freedom."

Chapter XII

Exciting Times

There is an old Chinese curse that goes, "May you live in interesting times." We are living in very interesting, potentially exciting times—more exciting than we realise—and whether this is a curse or a blessing depends on how we respond.

We are in the midst of a quantum change. Throughout the ages people have visited us, speaking of things that are going to happen, and we have not believed them. In fact, we have often become very upset and have killed them because we did not want to be disturbed. We maintain that we would like to feel happier, but we want things to move at a speed that is comfortable to us, one which we still feel we can control.

When Jesus spoke of the changes he foresaw, we crucified him. We did something similar to Socrates and we burned many people at the stake who told us things we were not prepared to hear. One of them was a woman who lived in England in the fifteenth century. She was not anyone very special; in fact, she was really quite ordinary. She was known as Mother Shipton and she predicted things that are happening in our lifetime. Her manuscripts are still available and indicate that in the fifteenth century she was saying, among other things, that we were going to fly through the air in machines and that women would cut their hair, wear trousers, and ride on motor bikes. Comparable predictions were made by the Egyptians, the Book of Revelations, Edgar Cayce, the Mayans and other people.

The events that have been prophesied are starting to happen. Things that have not been considered "real" in the past are now being commonly accepted. People on the leading edge of scientific exploration are beginning to realise this, and while many conventional scientists, particularly in the medical community, continue to resist, there are still many breakthroughs. For instance, on the European continent, homeopathy has become widely accepted, as well as other alternative healing methods.

Physicists are postulating scientific theories that mystics have declared for centuries. But even these changes still belong to a mode of life that we have known for thousands of years. There is a shift coming that is far beyond anything we have imagined possible and that heralds the beginning of a totally new way of living.

Most of the predictions seem to stop around 2012. This is because what will occur after that time is indescribable. They had no way of talking to us about what would happen and now that time is almost upon us. Reality as we know it is melting down, changing, shifting far beyond what we ever expected.

All our ways of living are based on what we have been told. Now that is simple to say, but it is almost impossible to get a glimpse of how powerful this conditioning is. If you are brought up in a culture that thinks a woman is beautiful if she is fat, most of the women in that country will be fat. If you are brought up in a country where you are admired and accepted if you are thin, you are more likely to be thin, especially when you are young. There are countries where people are honoured as they mature and they become more intelligent as they grow older. In other countries, as you age you are retired, are looked upon as a burden and so you become a burden and wither away.

There are tribes where it is accepted that you reach your

maximum athletic performance at the age of sixty; until then you are not considered to be at your best. These examples have been documented, yet they are not given much recognition because nobody, with our present way of looking at things, can explain these phenomena. These things are not due to diet, altitude or genetic make–up. They are a result of attitude, of belief systems.

When something is found to be possible that was previously thought to be impossible, it suddenly starts to occur all over the world. In the past, we rarely heard of people who had experienced spontaneous healing from illnesses that were said to be terminal. Now, many people are having this experience. We used to hear only occasionally about anyone who had clinically died and been brought back to life. Many cases have now been documented and the people who have had this experience tell us that we will not die. Thousands of people are saying, "We do not die when the body stops functioning." Of course, Zen and Hindu masters have been saying this for thousands of years. Bankai said, "We are not born, we will not die."

These things are beginning to integrate into our everyday life. The structure as we know it is starting to collapse and the predictors say this, too, is part of the design. The Book of Revelations states there will be plague, pestilence and famine, and that the weather will alter radically. The weather is changing all over the world— global warming, El Niño, La Niña are having radical effects on the climate. We have more indescribable and incurable illnesses than we have ever had. Strange, virulent viruses are appearing regularly; epidemics are spreading. It is all happening.

Everything is starting to shake. Deep down, we are beginning to recognise that what we have taken for granted is no longer secure. A phrase in the English language used to be "as safe as a bank." In recent years, some of the oldest, most established international banking institutions have collapsed.

The most significant shift, however, will not be with these material things. The greatest change will be in our experience of reality, in our consciousness and it is beginning to happen for many people all over the world.

There really is no easy way to explain a shift in consciousness. It means that the person who is looking at reality, the one you are familiar with, the one you call "I" is going to be very different. The difference is not only occurring in what the "I" sees and experiences, the fundamental "I" itself is starting to change. People who spend time in meditation are experiencing this essential shift. It is not simply a deviation in what we have called external reality— the seer is transforming.

Everything is affecting everything else, even in places we previously never considered it possible. Research scientists are speculating on how the human personality influences the way computers function. Anyone with a computer can probably report many instances of programs crashing when they feel out of sorts or in tension. Studies have indicated that a supposedly "non–feeling" robot will repeatedly, more frequently than random chance would predict, return to be in the section of an experimental cage where there are young animals.

Other research reflects on the relationship between doctor, diagnosis and patient. There is some indication that the illness you have and its degree of severity may be influenced by the doctor who treats you, the diagnosis they make and their expectation of your recovery. Some doctors have many cancer patients and others have very few in their practice. This may be influenced by the expectations the doctor has of identifying a body of symptoms as cancer rather than something else.

A well–known physicist discovered a particle for which he had been searching for years and when he found it, scientific researchers in different parts of world found it also, almost simultaneously. He says that he now suspects that this particle did not exist until he went looking for it. The implication here is that existence responded to his search and his seeking created the discovery. We do create our own lives. If you think and believe something strongly enough, it will happen. If you become obsessed either with not having cancer or with having it, you may get it.

The mind is incredibly powerful. There are people on the planet who can move things without touching them, merely by focusing their minds. Fortunately, most of us do not know how to focus our minds so effectively, otherwise we would be in all sorts of trouble. Yet we do focus our minds in many ways that impact everything.

In more practical terms, how does all this affect your life here and now? I am suggesting to you that any misery you are experiencing, without you realising it, is being created by you. You do not need to create any more pain and you might never be unhappy again. That is truly possible. I am not saying it is likely to happen, but I am not ruling out the possibility. If I were to say that it is not possible, I would be adding to the human tendency to be closed to something unexpected that might, in fact, be possible. I know this could be true, but I am not suggesting you believe me; just stay open and allow for this possibility. Your life could change *now*—totally, utterly and completely.

The difficulty with change, of course, is that in order to attain it, you have to change. Most people want change to happen without actually changing anything. They want to go back to the same house, the same partner, the same children, the same job, the same everything and be totally different. They want to eat the same unhealthy foods, take in unhealthy substances and be healthier. They want to go on avoiding truth, yet feel free. Again, I am not saying this is impossible; perhaps change could happen this way, but it is most unlikely.

If you want change, you have to change. Change has to do with truth. It says in the Bible, "The truth will set you free." And the truth *can* set you free, but it can generate a great deal of chaos in the process. The entire structure we have based our lives upon is built on lies. Fundamental lies are of the following type: Governments will keep you safe, doctors will keep you healthy, psychiatrists will keep you happy and marriage lasts forever. None of this is true. It is all based on a concept that we have created on planet Earth—the belief that life can be safe, secure and predictable.

This concept is false. This thing we call safety does not exist anywhere in the universe. We have created it because we want it to be true. Most of us have spent our entire lives devoted to this idea, yet we probably do not know one person, nor have we read or heard about anyone who has attained this state. No matter how famous, no matter how wealthy or powerful, no one can have a life that is safe, secure and predictable. No one. Thousands of people die every day who were not expecting to die. They go to the doctor because they think they have indigestion and discover that their bowels are riddled with cancer. There is no predictability. There is no happiness based on the outside and no guarantee of happiness in the future. The future is totally uncertain.

The Kingdom of God is within, now, in everyone. Right now. You have forgotten how to access it because you have gotten lost in the mind. The mind keeps telling you how you are going to be safe, secure and how you can predict life. But you are not safe, you are not secure, and there is no predictability. The moment you accept this totally, here and now, you are in that indescribable inner state.

Jesus said, "Take no thought of the morrow. Let the morrow take thought of itself." Be here, now. Do not go to your thoughts, for as soon as you think, you are in hell. The mind is itself a negative process. It creates a huge data bank of all the things that can possibly go wrong based on the past, and that is usually the way we live—hoping that something will go right, but mostly expecting the worst and trying to avoid what can go wrong.

When you find the knack of disconnecting from your mind—not stopping it, disconnecting from it—you are instantly in bliss, a state that is beyond description.

Misery is sourced in the mind because the mind continually accesses the past and projects it onto a possible future. Nothing new is possible in this context.

When you disconnect from the past and the future, something indescribable occurs. You realise, not believe, but know from your own experience, that you are not your body. You know that you are not your mind and you are not your emotions. You are in a recycled vehicle made of bits of your mother, bits of your father, bits of their parents, bits of the nuclear atomic particles that are released every time we let a bomb go off. The body is made up of all these bits and more. It is not you. You are the one who knows you have a body. The body does not know it has a body. The eye does not know it can see.

You are the one who knows that you have a body, a mind and emotions. You are in a highly unstable vehicle. It gets set off by illogical things. It can get upset about the same thing again and again for its entire life. It never seems to learn. It is as though it has an allergy and when somebody says something, it gets upset. No one has hurt it, no one has damaged it; it just did not want to hear what was said, so it gets upset.

It is not you who is upset. Your mind heard something and created a reaction in the body and the emotions. The essential you is the one who can watch the reaction.

However, you forget to watch; you get caught up in it and you think that you are angry. *You* are not angry. The body, mind and emotions have become disturbed, chemicals have been released and there is nothing you can do about it.

Let us imagine that someone accuses you of stealing something and they become angry. You feel very upset at being accused and then the person finds that what they thought you had taken is in their pocket. They say, "Oh, I'm sorry! It wasn't you at all." Yet you continue to feel upset; your body and mind are still disturbed. It is all over, but the chemicals are still running through your system and you are still shaking and thinking about it. But all that is not you, that is your system. You can detach and watch the entire process.

Consider yourself in this situation that happened to me. I picked up a beautiful new car many years ago and I went directly to a concert and left it parked there. When I came out of the performance I saw that someone had taken a knife all the way down the side of the car, ripping off the paint and actually damaging the metal beneath. I had been looking forward to coming out and being with my beautiful new car. What a shock!

Imagine how you might have felt in this situation. If you are present, if you are there, if you do not get caught up in the turmoil of the mind, the disturbance in the body, and the chaos of the emotions, what you have is a fact—not a problem. A fact. The facts are, you have to take the car in for repair and attend to the insurance and all the practical details. These are all facts. But you would probably not leave it there; you would think about it for the rest of the day, feeling upset and angry with the person who had done it. Yet there is another way to be with this kind of incident. There is the possibility of accepting what is—"This is it"—and going on with your day, your life.

It is possible to live these moments of life as facts, not as problems. If your partner has decided they want to live with someone else, this is not a problem—it is a fact. If only you could recognise this, you would be on the way to freedom. Then, the next step—and I know this is a big step—is to realise that nothing is ever against you. You are always getting what you need to become more awake, more yourself. But you usually want what you want and you reject what comes to you when it does not fit your desires. That rejection, that "no," that fight, is your prison, your misery.

Take a moment to tune in to yourself now. Forget what you have been reading and be with you. What are you feeling? What is going on with you right now? Let yourself be easy with this, because you do not have to change. You do not have to believe or agree or disagree. Simply take a look for yourself. Do you feel anything? Does this resonate with you in any way?

I am suggesting to you that you can be different right now. It is possible for you to shed your misery and allow your bliss. It is entirely up to you. Anything is possible. Anything.

"Waking up is seeing yourself just as you are,
not as you would like to be nor
as you are afraid you might be."

Chapter XIII
Beyond Choosing

The persistent experience of misery in life is not created by significant events or tragedies, but by our unconscious reactions to the ordinary, everyday incidents of our lives. One of the most common ways we lock ourselves up in life is through our attachment to wanting what we want. Practically everything in our lives is a desire. We may call it a choice, yet that is often just another word for a demand. We go about our lives demanding the world be the way we want it.

Imagine yourself in this situation. You are on holiday and you come down to breakfast to find that what you want is not being served. You ask for bread and if there is no bread, you might become upset, perhaps angry. *You* created that feeling of distress—not the lack of bread, not the waiters, not the people running the restaurant. You did that to yourself. If you had felt a preference for bread rather than a demand for it, when it is not available, there would be no distress.

We create our own misery by resisting what is in front of us. A preference is different from a demand in that we recognise what we want without being attached to having it. Of course we would all prefer to be comfortable, but if that is not feasible in the circumstances, we can be as total as possible with things as they are.

Here is another example. I recently bought a sarong and I went through many of them to select the very best one. I brought it home, opened it and discovered that I had chosen one with marks on it, and the place where I had bought it was many miles away. Earlier in my life, I would have tortured myself with the thought that I now had the wrong one and I would have literally suffered with the consequences of that—either to go through the discomfort of taking a taxi a great distance to change it, or to put up with it and feel unhappy. I think you all will recognise this kind of incident. This is how hell is created, many times in the course of a day.

In the past, there was often little difference for me

between losing a $100,000 investment or discovering a dirt mark on a sarong. It was the same thing, the same torture inside, the same desolation in not having what is desired.

I have discovered that the way to unlock this self–inflicted pattern of torture is to be there with the feelings. You do not want the torture, so you keep running away from the distress. But it does not go away. The alternative is to be present and feel it, now, as it is happening. It is the same with jealousy or any feeling you do not want to experience. Be there and have the feeling even though you do not know how long it will last. When you do not avoid or energise the feelings by dwelling on them or making them important, they will start to fade away on their own.

When I think about my own spiritual journey, it has really never been about being "spiritual." Finding peace has had nothing to do with discovering other dimensions or becoming enlightened. It has been about being here in each moment and when I have gone unconscious, saying, "Oh— slipped up there," and beginning anew, right now, present in this moment, accepting what is. At any time we can always start again. And again.

Someone told me that he once threw an expensive movie camera into a lake in a fury because it did not work the way he wanted. I have done similar things; most of us have. That energy comes and you explode. One day I started to be with that feeling and *not* act it out and eventually it started to fade. The preference is still there to have things be the way I might want, but now there is no contraction when life does not happen as I would like it to. There is no choice, no demand.

When we are ready to give up our demands we will find our freedom. If we want to be free and continue to insist on having what we want, we will never be free. We may say we want to be free, that we do not want the anger or the disturbance, but still, we continue to want what we want. We still want our way and the feeling of discontent will always flow from that demand, no matter how slight it may seem.

We carry so many demands on life. We demand that people treat us the way we want to be treated; that we be seen the way we want to be seen; that people give us what we want; that they don't give us what we don't want. This is the very heart of our misery.

We demand what we want, not what we need. Perhaps you may need to get upset even though it may feel uncomfortable. You may need to be upset so you can be with your distress and go deeper into it in order for it to complete itself. Something has become locked up inside you, probably having something to do with the past, and you have to keep opening to it in order to come to a place of balance. You do not want the pain and so you focus on what you want instead of what is actually here, in front of you. Now.

Sometimes people say they have difficulty trusting other people. They are really saying, "I demand that you be trustworthy—according to my standards." Once again, it is a demand. "I demand that you treat me this way. I demand that existence be the way I want. I demand that I don't get ill. I demand that I am happy. I demand that the person I am with is faithful to me. I demand that my mother treat me the way I want. I demand that my children . . . ." *Everything that we are upset about arises from holding a demand.* Everything.

I have met people with quadriplegic injury who are happy and I have met people with an ache in their wrist who are very miserable. The difference between them has to do with acceptance and nonacceptance. We know a man who dived off a pier into water that was not as deep as he had expected and he severed his spine. When we met him, he was the life of a conference we were holding. He could not move any part of his body except his mouth to speak, and he also had some slight facial expression. He was pushed everywhere and had his neck held up all the time. Yet he was laughing and joking. He had no demand that life be any different than it was. He accepted the way he was.

Some people have an ache and they demand it to be different. Preferring it to be different is something else. Preference goes like this: "I prefer this to be different. However, it is the way it is and I'll take care of it. What can't be taken care of I accept." Even "I accept" is in the way. It simply is! That is the way it is.

Demanding things from life may produce results on one level, but those results will never deeply satisfy you. I keep returning to the phrase that says out of love comes love. Only from love can love arise. You may have made beautiful things. But do they fulfill you? I mean really *fulfill* you. When you create something from a demand, out of pressure from the will, from the desire to have something be the way you want it, there is never a sense of enduring fulfillment upon completion.

Imagine that you want a garden landscaped exactly to your specifications and you use your will to force it to happen. The trees and flowers might be put in the right place but it will probably lack a feeling of peace. There may be perfection, but not love. When you create out of love, out of the flow of existence, fulfillment streams through you.

We can go to another level with this. Each of us is a genius in our own way; we each register things that other people do not see or hear or sense. When one of us shares what we see with other people, they may think they understand what we are saying, but really, they do not. We each see other levels of possibility in a situation of which others may not be aware. If you are an artist, perhaps a filmmaker, you might be shooting a scene and you say, "I want it this way." The film crew may think they know what you are attempting to create, but essentially, they do not, because they do not have your eye, your perfection about things. Their interpretation of what you want will be different, perhaps only in a subtle way. You will be in distress with this if you are attached to the outcome.

We become stuck when we are identified with the outcome. If we would go to preference, which says, "I would really love this to be the way I can see it, if it is appropriate . . . ," if we use no pressure, no will, then we will have no misery about it. It might be the way we want or it might be different, but either way it will flow from us.

It is the same thing for me when I talk to groups. Usually people only see a fraction of the depth of which I am attempting to speak. I assume some of the responsibility for that as it might have something to do with how I am expressing myself. But I do not feel guilty or upset about it, because my whole life, every moment, is about being more aware and finding ways to share that with people. When I am in a group I am absolutely total with everything, and when I leave, I have no regret about what may not have been understood. I was total, but I was not identified with an outcome.

Anything created out of the will, out of contraction and control, never produces an enduring sense of satisfaction and contentment. Rather, your meditation can be in each moment, being as sensitive and choiceless as possible. When you are present, you can sense a demand coming up in you because you can feel yourself contracting, you can feel the tension inside you. Catch it as early as possible and then ask, "Now what am I demanding or resisting?" and just be there with it. Give yourself the experiment of going for your maximum potential with love and sensitivity, without demand or control. See if you can invite what you would most like in each moment and allow it to emerge without interference.

Chapter XIV

Alive With Silence

A time of silence is coming—a silence that is totally alive and radiant with acceptance and infuses everything we do. Such a sense of stillness and peace is already happening for many people. Often we become uncomfortable with the stillness because we have been busy and in so much turmoil. When we feel the quiet we may think that we are missing or avoiding something. The time is coming when we will be available to flow with the stillness and give up looking for things to work on.

A time is coming when it will be appropriate to be much softer and more gentle with ourselves. If something goes out of balance, we can gently call it to the surface of our consciousness and be more accepting of ourselves rather than beating ourselves up.

Just as everything is one, everything is also separate, equally. Each part of you—your mind, your body, your feelings—has a consciousness of its own and is complete in itself. If any part is distressed, it needs to be cared for, loved back into balance, not blamed. For example, when part of your body is not functioning the way you would like it to, there are two aspects to this. Of course, you are responsible for how you are treating your body—being stressed, not eating or exercising properly; that is one aspect. But that part of you also needs to be loved and cared for, no matter how you see it. You only have two choices—you can either bless that part or curse it.

We tend to blame and curse ourselves in ways that reflect how we were treated as children. If we were not behaving the way adults wanted us to do, we were shouted at, blamed and punished. Now, as adults, we have continued this habit with ourselves and it perpetuates the damage. Consider, instead, embracing the parts of you that feel out of balance, that are not functioning at their optimum. Only love heals.

Unconditional love is capable of seeing the source of who we are; it does not get caught up in the behaviour. We all have behaviours that we would prefer to be different. Through our life experiences, unaware choices, our conditioning and life circumstances, we have developed these patterns. This behaviour needs not to be condemned, it needs to be loved back into balance.

Take a moment to imagine the sound of running water, of a dancing stream. Now imagine that is the flow of your life—it is moving, it is dancing. Life is moving on its own. In this stream there are a few rocks or roots stuck in the mud, just as there may be things stuck or a bit difficult in your life—but the stream is running. Identify the rocks, be aware of them, be with them and they will dissolve. Everything is fine.

In the stream of life you have some difficulties, and usually, these difficulties are determined by anything you are resisting, that you are not allowing to be the way they are. The stream of life is running and you hit a rock, you want something to be the way you want it to be. That willfulness solidifies something in you that turns it into a rock, an obstruction to the flow of life. Having a preference for things to be the way you would like them to be is natural. But as soon as you make them a choice, you are in misery. The stream of life bumps up against your resistance.

The resistance is not logical. Seeing it, being with it, allowing it will make it dissolve and then the stream of life can move on, unobstructed. You can feel the flow of life, you can feel the stream is carrying you if you do not hold on to the shore. You can let go of holding; nothing is safe, nothing is secure, nothing is predictable, but when you let yourself into the flow of life, you are very alive.

Take a moment to look at where you are holding on to things in your life, clinging to the riverbank, grabbing at the roots. See if you can feel the image. When you are in the stream, when you are in the river, flowing, there is no resistance. You and the river are one. You and life are one. If you grab out for a root along the sides, if you make a demand— "This is the way I want it"—you can feel the river bumping up against you.

Do not hold on and you are back in the stream of life. If you need that root, it will float with you. It is time to let the river carry you, time to be with everything, gently. There is no need to be against the roots and rocks or against yourself for holding on to them. Allow the stream to float you. Be with the movement and with the stillness. It is all there for you.

Chapter XV
Waking Up – It's Not What You Think

For forty years I travelled all over the world, actively seeking freedom. I have gone down many paths, been with many acclaimed teachers and gurus and experimented with most of the known techniques for awakening. I have not seen anything work effectively. My conclusion is that nothing on the outside works. No method, no technique, no teaching in itself leads to freedom or awakening.

Every path has a practice. The tradition in Zen is to meditate for eighteen hours a day for twenty, thirty or forty years and yet, hardly anything happens for anyone. I also did nothing but sit for years. One year I sat for eighteen hours a day, and for eight years I sat for six hours a day.

While sitting did bring me something, it did not bring me freedom. *Nothing on the outside, in itself, sets you free.*

Then suddenly one day, something did work for me. Something clicked and it was not because of anything I had been doing or not doing. What happened did not come from the outside. It was inside me. At the same time that I found it was from the inside, I also discovered that it was not the inside or the outside—all distinctions had blurred.

When this inexplicable "click" happens, and it can happen to anyone, you realise the profundity in what has been said by people who have awakened. You come in touch with everything, including all the apparent paradoxes, and you see clearly what they mean at an entirely new depth. You know, not with your mind, but from your own experience. It is something indescribable. In Zen it is said that usually when you reach this place you simply laugh, because at the moment it happens, you realise you knew it all the time. But you had been trying to understand it with the mind and it is not about understanding.

All of our attempts to understand are something of a trip. I am using the word "trip" to mean the efforts of someone to influence others to see reality their way. But awakening is a pathless path; it is not about a way. Most people, groups and organisations are on some type of trip. There is the New Age, the spiritual, the guru trip and many others. Anything we follow, anything we think is going to move us to wake up or be free is a trip, a fixed idea in which we are invested. Any ideas we might be thinking about enlightenment are not true, because awakening is not about thinking. If we can think it, it is not that.

Still, there is something. It is nothing and it is everything. It cannot be spoken. It is a state of being that is beyond description. But we have assigned it many names: peace, godliness, harmony, the source. It is there to be experienced when we give up understanding. When we stop trying, we discover it has been there all the time. We have been attempting to fit it into the limitation of what we thought it was but the mind cannot recognise it. When we disconnect from the mind and allow, we are there.

Most of the people who have attained this state of awakening say there is nothing we can do to get there. We can meditate for as long as we like; we can make ourselves aware or be as conscious as possible, but it really does not matter what we do. We cannot "do" anything to reach this state.

People who have attained it have been asked, "When and how did this state happen to you?" Buddha was known to say that it happened suddenly, after twelve years of total trying. Gurdjieff responded that he was with every master he could find. Bankai spent thirty years sitting on one piece of stone, waiting. Ask U. G. Krishnamurti, who is still alive, and he is likely to tell us not to look for it; that it's a calamity, and there is nothing we can do anyway. You may ask again, "But how did you get there?" and U. G. would probably say that it's irrelevant. Yet take a look into his life. He searched and searched and something happened when he gave up.

When we truly give up it seems that there is suddenly something—we could call it a universal consciousness. We disappear into the One. It is not, though, what the New Age means when they say, "We are the One." The New Age tends to put the idea of oneness in the way. It *is* the One, but not what the *ego–mind* thinks it is.

When we say "It is the One," it is as though there is a One, but the truth is, there is not. There is nothing—and yet there is "the One." The mind cannot understand that. *The mind cannot understand paradoxes. It cannot understand anything. It only thinks it can.* When you disconnect from the mind, something else is able to happen.

I know of an extreme example that occurred to a man who was in one of my groups many years ago. His name is John Wren–Lewis. At the time that I first knew him, he was very rational and scientific. He thought mysticism and everything of that sort was complete nonsense. He and his wife, Ann Faraday, were travelling in

Thailand on a bus, where they were given some poisoned candy by a man who intended to rob them. Unaware of the danger, John ate the candy and he lost consciousness— essentially, he died and then came back to life. But when he came back, he had a completely different sense of everything.

He had been a serious and well–respected scientist before this experience. When he came back, he was able to perceive a much greater, more expanded level of reality than he had ever known through his scientific perspective. We spent a weekend together chatting about his experience and he described it this way.

"I call it the radiant darkness, but it is not dark. The moment I realised the darkness was there, I realised it has always been there. When I came back, I was expecting it to go, but it didn't disappear. All that happened was that I became less aware of it in some situations and more aware of it in others. It seems to have something to do with my being present and my allowing and my honesty. If I put anything in the way of it, I lost touch with it." Now he reports that he lives in this state continuously.

These examples of waking up are often very different from what is expected. Another example is someone in Australia, whom I have known for many years. He was a yoga teacher but he was not doing anything as spiritual as teaching yoga when he woke up. He was loading very large pieces of wood onto a truck and one fell off. It was 20 feet long by 12 inches by 5 inches, and it hit him hard, on the head. As he was dying, he said to himself, "This is wonderful because after all this yoga I've done, it's a certainty I'm going to get enlightened." He was slipping away when he had the thought, "My wife is going to be unhappy if I don't go home." The next wonderful thought he had was, ". . . And I didn't do the dishes and I haven't finished the garden." Then a voice said, "If you want to go back, step to the left." So he did, and he came back as they were pumping his chest, trying to revive him.

I am not recommending being knocked out by huge pieces of lumber or eating drugged sweets as methods to wake up. There is really nothing we can do to attain this state, because the state is here now and anything we do is in the way; all trying takes us further from where we really are. It is here right now and it is indescribable. Searching and striving take us away from the present moment.

We can never think it and we can never experience it because it is not separate from ourselves. It is not an experience but it is with each one of us, now.

If we think it is something else, we have just taken a step to the left. If we do some sort of discipline that we believe will bring us closer to it, we have just taken ten steps to the left. It is here and it is now, exactly as we are. If we would live our truth to ourselves and to others, we would realise this. If we do anything in order to wake up, even if we meditate to awaken, rather than for the fullness of the meditation, we are not accepting the way we are. We are indicating that we want to be better, to be different and we are rejecting how we are now. This is diametrically opposed to what is needed to realise this harmony. When we recognise and accept that "This Is It"—the way we and everything is right now is all there is—we are on the threshold of our freedom.

Whatever this state is, it is not what our mind thinks it is. "Thou art That." We are in this state always, but we do not experience it when we think that it is *something*, or when we are chasing somewhere to find it, or when we think we have to work and maintain a discipline to attain it. Anything we do from the mind is all to do with the mind. It has nothing to do with anything else.

When awakening happens, it occurs on its own, unstimulated and unaware of itself. It has no thought, it has no feeling. It has nothing. It is awareness but it has no awareness of awareness. *It just is*. Until the phone rings or the dog barks or somebody asks a question—then a response happens. Not a reaction, not an idea, not a thought—a response. Something flows out of the moment, but you are not using your will to do it. It seems to originate in some natural, unplanned part of you.

It is similar to the times when you may have been involved in an activity, perhaps dancing, and you were so engaged and quick and graceful you were not thinking about what you were doing—you *were* the dance. Someone might comment, "That was some great dancing you did," but you feel that you cannot say, "I did that," because in those moments you were so total, so involved, that there was no sense of self. A response to the situation happened directly through you. The dance did you.

When that state of emptiness is reached, you *are* a response. If the system reacts in some way, you can watch the system as though it is someone else. If it should become angry, if it should be disturbed, you can say, "This system is disturbed." You recognise there is nothing you can do about it and there really is no problem. Whatever it is, it will pass. If you do anything to escape from this, if you meditate in order to avoid the feelings you are having or to attain a higher state, you are rejecting what is actually happening. The gateway to the next level of what we each need is in this moment—exactly as it is.

This means that whatever you are experiencing, you need to feel it. If you are angry, you need to be angry. I do not mean for you to act out the anger on someone else, nor does it mean forcing it inside. If you will allow your anger and be there and be present, you will find your anger begins to fade. You do not do the anger. The anger does you. This is true of everything.

On one level, being awake is about the experience of being totally open and available to everyone and everything. It is an openness that is difficult to describe, but is something like this: If you are open and unconditional when you meet someone, something will happen in you. You are a response to something that is happening.

You feel hungry, so you eat; or you hear the birds and you think, "I'd like to go for a walk." You go for a walk, then you see someone who is sad, and you are touched by this sadness. So you sit down beside them and they want to talk. Still you are doing nothing. Response is happening through you. None of your actions come from your will. Existence functions this way. Things keep happening if you are available to see, feel and respond. With greater levels of sensitivity, you start perceiving all sorts of things that are going on and you simply respond. Life flows on its own. There is a Zen saying that goes, "When I am tired, I sleep; when I am hungry, I eat." Life is whatever is happening—right now, in this moment.

On another level there is nothing called experience, there is no watcher. Now, do not try to understand this, but on this level you have become everything. If you go out of that to be the experiencer, you are separate. You were the drop. Now you have become the ocean. And the memory of the drop is also the experience of the ocean.

It is a matter of disconnecting from your patterns and all the things that have given you an identity. If all this goes, who is there? You do not know how you are going to be. But you are going to be there one day. No matter what you do, how much you resist, one day you are going to wake up. It is just a matter of how long you want to take. It could happen right now.

Chapter XVI
Being Together – A Vision of the Possible

Many of us have dreamed of the possibilities of living together in communion—sharing, speaking and living in truth. I have a sense of what a community of all of us could be like. I invite you to join me in imagining this possibility.

I see that we would be living in something similar to the tradition of a monastery or an ashram, where the priority is on moment–to–moment awareness. Unlike most ashrams though, instead of performing rituals or doing serious things, we would be living, having fun and playing—with awareness. There would be an invitation to move to ever deepening levels of presence in all that we do—every task, every human interaction and every moment we may spend alone.

The foundation for everything would be based on people who are ready to be responsible. The only way to go beyond the restrictions of how we have lived as human beings is to be responsible for ourselves, at every level. That includes the willingness to go to the source of our disturbance instead of blaming someone else. In fact, it might just be the opposite—when we are disturbed, instead of blaming others, we would thank them for helping us to find that place in ourselves that was not in balance.

As we operate out of responsibility, there would be no processing, as such. Processing is what we do to avoid experiencing the moment. We would not put out anger or other negative emotions, nor would we hold anything inside. It entails disconnecting from anger, complaint, jealousy— from all emotions. We are just with the disturbance or upset that is created inside. We are aware of it, present with it, not blaming and not suppressing anything.

Everyone would be involved in all the household tasks, the cleaning, the food preparation, the shopping. If enough of us want to meditate totally, we hire some people to do the basic things. Meditation is the priority. If possible, we do all our own practical things as a meditation. There is no fixed program, everything stays loose, so that if you feel to meditate at any time, if you feel that energy coming, you honour it in that moment. Regarding food, the diet would consist of live, uncooked foods and there is no meat. The encouragement is for you to be much more conscious of your eating habits.

The level of awareness is such that when you put a vase of flowers down, you know exactly where you are placing it. You look at the surface on which you are putting it and feel where it is appropriate to be placed. You are aware that the flowers, the vase and the table all have consciousness. You put things away in drawers consciously. You do everything with an inclusive awareness.

You are aware of each other at all times. This does not mean just on the surface of consciousness—you may not be talking to or looking at anyone—yet now you are living in an awareness that includes everyone, all the time. Imagine a space where the barriers we maintain between ourselves are all down. Where we are *for* each other. As anyone gets into difficulty with themselves or as they move to another level where they may feel disoriented, we are all *with* them. Everything that happens is part of all of us.

If there are couples, they are not exclusive. That does not mean they have to spend time with other people, rather that they are available to themselves and any possibility that is appropriate, moment to moment. No one excludes anyone. You are here to enjoy yourself, to have a good time and to be available for another level of your consciousness, always.

There is no trying or forcing, no tension to make anything happen. You are open to any support, in any form, on any level, at any time.

I sense that there is real tenderness with ourselves and each other—deep, caring support. If somebody starts to go into something unknown, they are on their own—*and* they have support. They have space to be, a physical space to be on their own, and they are constantly supported, without interference. There is support and all the space needed to go into aloneness.

Without any trying or doing, there is a constant availability and openness for another level of consciousness, an abiding invitation in everyone. If the sense of reality starts to shift, that becomes the priority, whatever you may be doing. You stop and stay with that shift, that movement.

There is no discipline from the outside. Everything comes from the inside, from consciousness. You are tidy, not as a rule, not to please anyone, but out of your own consciousness. Wherever you place anything, you put it there with awareness. Constant, gentle reminders of our unconscious patterns are offered among us all about posture, about facial expressions, how we dress, tone of voice and any other habits. They are soft, supportive reminders, all of us are together in this. We are disconnecting from competition, disconnecting from approval, disconnecting from the fear of disapproval. There is a total dissolving of all levels of hierarchy, of authority. Everyone is taking responsibility.

There are no morals, no taboos, no rules. There is only consciousness, sensitivity and appropriateness. We are there to support each other not to go over the top of ourselves and not to hold back, to be there, present to each moment. When a reminder is offered, feedback is received with an instantaneous response, an openness and availability, not a reaction. There is no attacking, no defending, no cutting off. Instead there is a readiness to see if that feedback, that remark, is appropriate.

There is complete, total honesty. If conflicts arise in any way that do not resolve easily between the people involved, a meeting is called with everyone, instantly. Nothing is left incomplete or postponed until later. Everything happens in the moment. There are no set times for anything—to eat, to sleep, to play. We each listen to our system to know when anything is appropriate for ourselves.

There is total togetherness and total aloneness. If we connect with someone in the community, we stay open to experiment with being one together, without being exclusive, allowing ourselves to go to a depth within ourself and the other that we may never have dared to experience before.

See if you can just float gently with this. The difficulty

is that you are normally locked into *doing*. It may look as though you are not doing, but you *are* doing things all the time. You are making things happen, or avoiding something or holding back. What I am talking about is totally the opposite. It is about being in each moment, *being here*, sharing what is there, and being so open that there is no struggle when someone has something to say to you. You are totally there with gratitude: "Thank you for reminding me." No defense, no reacting, just keep floating.

You become increasingly sensitive to who you are, moment by moment. More and more you drop into what is actually happening for you in each moment. There is no pretense in any way. It is just about being right in this moment and saying, "Now this is what is going on with me. Right now. This is what is happening." And so you are not hiding anything, you are not inflating anything, you are just there with you. And then you are with everything and everyone else, as well.

Creating a physical community somewhere where we could all be together would be wonderful, but we do not need to wait. We could all be living this way, right now, right here.

You can start your life now.

Chapter XVII

All the Way Home – To Ourselves

When I meet someone, it is as though I am meeting my brother or my sister. We meet with an intimacy that is not usually experienced on this planet. It is so intimate that there really is no separation between us. Of course, there is no way of explaining this because we *are* separate, we *are* in separate bodies; but, to me, we are the same source. I do not mean that we come from the same source. We *are* the same source.

We have all been crippled in some way at birth. It is as if we had a stroke or a type of aberration as we entered this dimension. I have spent my whole life correcting this kind of crippling and now it has been corrected. Most people are still living inside that impairment. When we meet, we meet as brother and sister, but we do not recognise each other that way because most of us still exist behind the injury that has created the illusion of separateness.

As you read this, consider this possibility. Your body is damaged, your brain is damaged, your emotions are damaged, but you are perfect. Nothing has happened to you, but you do not recognise this because you do not know how to access yourself directly. You do not know how to be with your source. You access yourself through your damaged body, your damaged mind and your damaged emotions. You see yourself that way and you think that is who you are. But that is not who you are.

I have gotten where I am through . . . the words that come to me are blessing, luck, coincidence and hard work. I do not know exactly how I got here. I do not actually know how this waking up has happened, but as a result, I see you as you really are. You do not see yourself as you are. You see yourself through your damaged faculties, and consequently, you experience yourself through your behaviour, not directly.

For most of you, what I am saying is beyond the framework of your experience. You might think you understand it, but you can only put what you hear in a context you already know. You have not truly realised that you are pure spirit. If you were to realise that you are pure spirit, not as an idea nor as a belief, but as a direct knowing, you would feel no discomfort, no disturbance. You would have no fear, ever, at any time. If you believe me about this, it will not make any difference to you; in fact, belief gets in the way. Rather, listen to what I am offering and see if you can open to it as an hypothesis. You are spirit and you are out of touch with this because you have been damaged.

A man I know has hurt his feet badly, but inside he is not damaged. He cannot get around the way he used to; in fact, for a while he could not get around at all and he had to use a wheelchair. But that had nothing to with him. That was about his feet. He could not do the things he had done in the past—running or playing or doing sports—because of the injury to his feet, but that had nothing to do with him.

You have a body that is out of balance, a mind that is in distress, emotions that are in turmoil, but all that has nothing to do with you. If you identify with them, you feel crippled and less than whole. But that is not you.

It helps to become more aware of how the mind functions, because the body and emotions follow the mind. When you become aware of this process you are less likely to become involved in it. Do not take it seriously, rather allow the observer in you to notice, "Oh, a negative thought just happened." The mind thought negatively; you are not negative, your system went into a pattern. Allow yourself to see it more clearly and keep disconnecting from the function of the mind. You become angry—the mind has gone into malfunction. You are capable of seeing that you do not have to be angry. You can let the mind be angry and the body change its temperature and its vibration, but you do not have to go there. It is the same with any emotion.

You do not need to identify with your emotions and behaviour. You may say, "I am depressed," yet, *you* are not depressed. *You* cannot be depressed. What you are saying is that there is an imbalance in your mind that affects your body and emotions. But that is not you.

When you identify with feelings or behaviours, you believe they *are* you and you tend to become either lost in them or to work on changing them. In both cases you are avoiding simply experiencing them. You cannot change them; in fact, it is inappropriate to change any of it. All you need do is become more aware of the part of you—the watcher—who is aware that you feel depressed, or whatever you are feeling. Then you can start to identify with the watcher and not the watched.

I am beginning to experience myself as less personal with people, but it is actually with their behaviour, not who they really are. To me, it is as if most people are very beautiful beings who are dressing themselves as horribly as possible, on every level: physically, mentally, emotionally, spiritually.

I am interested in people's beauty, not the rags, the dirt, the problems they wear. Everyone is a beautiful, shining being— that is who I am interested in.

When you talk about your troubles, your pain and distress have nothing to do with who you are. That is what you are wearing. That is your outer form, and you are trying to deal with your outer form instead of dropping back to the purity of who you are inside.

Do not bother focusing attention on your behaviour because it has nothing to do with you. When you make yourself available to the possibility of your purity, of your essential being, all the other things drop away. In the meantime, you need to function through your behaviour, through your body, your mind and your emotions. It is important to be present and disconnect with all of that, even as you are functioning. Be there. Do not do anything to change, simply be there without judgment. Everything on the outside will then begin to find its balance.

My experience is that many people are, in fact, beginning to disconnect from their behaviour. As you do, you realise that in one way nothing has changed. You are still doing many of the old patterns, yet in another way, you now have some distance from your behaviour. You have let go of something that you felt was valuable at one time, but has not really supported you. With the letting go, you are healing, while at the same time, part of you is not really healing because it has never been sick.

As this happens, your behaviour begins to line up with your essential self and your judgments, both bad and good, will gradually dissolve. With that comes an empty space, a not–knowing space. All your life you have been trained to evaluate good or bad, right or wrong and to believe you then know where you are, because you have a reference point. If you let this go the duality disappears, the point of reference disappears, and then you do not know. If you want to feel safe and have a sense of knowing again, you are back in duality, right/wrong, good/bad. If you let it all go, you let the your ideas of the source go as well. Then you really do not know. But something replaces it that is indescribable. It is replaced by the "peace that passeth all understanding."

Take a moment now to see if you can identify your most prominent behaviour. What is the primary thought, feeling or action you go to automatically? If you distilled everything down, what would be the main theme in your life? Here are some suggestions to stimulate you: you may be predominantly angry, sorry for yourself, blaming, judging, or feeling helpless, insecure, afraid, superior or inferior. Not only is pessimism on that list, optimism is also there.

This is the pattern you drop into when you do not know what is going on, or when you feel disturbed or upset. You drop into this one place because you know it well. While it may not feel good, it offers the security of familiarity.

Keep looking, but not with your mind or your old eyes. Imagine looking at yourself through me, even though you do not know who I am. I have no judgment; whether you are a negative person or a positive person makes no difference to me. However, you judge all that. I see your value as a being, because "Thou art That." To me, you are the Kingdom of God. You have put this behaviour on top of your essence and it is not you.

See if you can just consider your unconscious behaviour as a fact. Of course, you would have a preference for it not to be there, but it is not wrong, it is not bad; it is simply a fact. This is what your life experience has brought you to. This is your cave—where you take yourself when it all feels too much; when you get angry or feel sorry for yourself. You go there simply because you know it. It is not comfortable, but you know it. It is the place you created for yourself as a child when it was almost impossible to live. Life was so painful, so disturbing, so bewildering that you created this behaviour to help yourself survive.

Imagine for a moment that you are an angry person or someone who tries to please others all the time. The anger or those attempts at approval, that is your cave. You are being invited to come out of your cave and as you do so, you are going to feel naked. You are going to feel vulnerable. You are being invited to come out of that place and start to experience yourself without that protection.

Some of you are sharing your source and some of you are sharing your behaviour. Let us take a look at this distinction. When you go to your cave you are feeling something. You may be feeling insecure, frightened, upset or unworthy. The question to consider is, how do you compensate for that? What is the behaviour you revert to in order to cover up what is really going on? Let us say you feel unworthy deep inside and you have a behaviour on the outside that might be acting superior. You might have fear on the inside and on the outside you behave aggressively.

These two things are always occurring simultaneously—what you are really feeling inside and the behaviour that you present to other people. I have heard people say that they were feeling insecure but their behaviour is to look together and rather cool. You do something like that, too. You have the essence of your inner experience and then you have what you put over that. Take a look at these two parts of yourself now. What is really going on inside and what do you show on the outside? Perhaps you show what you are. If you are afraid you show fear; if you are angry you show anger. Take a look. Is there a dichotomy? Do you pretend to be the opposite of what you feel?

On one level, you might know yourself fairly well. You know what you are doing and what you are covering up. Now check inside again. You have your cave and you have your behaviour. On a scale of 1 to 10, how effective is your behaviour? If you have given yourself a low number, consider why you keep doing the behaviour. You probably continue it because that is what you know. You would rather do something you recognise than be there, not knowing and feeling all that is inside when you have no reference point. Yet this is the invitation now—be with the not knowing and make yourself available to another level of possibility.

When you stop covering up what you are really feeling you allow yourself to drop back to the roots of your disturbance. You will find that, just as there is a distance between the covering behaviour and the disturbance, there is equally a distance between the roots of the disturbance and your essential self, your source. As you become aware of each level, you drop closer to the direct experience of your source.

First you see the behaviour. Then you decide to stop the behaviour and to drop into the origin of the disturbance, where you feel the part of you that is insecure. As you allow yourself to be there—present, experiencing the feelings you have been avoiding—you suddenly come back to the source.

You may experience the separation between the source and what you call yourself.

At the moment, many of you recognise that you do have a choice about whether you cover up your vulnerability or not. You get angry, you cover that up and you can see that you are creating this. As you stop creating it, suddenly you can let it go and drop to the source. When you drop into source, the "you" as you have known yourself to be, is gone. You have no separate identification. Do not try to understand that. The mind thinks it knows, but it does not. It can feel like death. Yet, as the Bible says, "unless you die and be reborn . . . ," until you are willing to let go of who you think you are, you are separate from source.

There are these levels to drop into: the behavioural cover–up, the root of the disturbance, and then the source. As you disconnect from one, you keep dropping back. Disconnect, drop down, and then . . . you are dancing naked in the moonlight, realising you are the grass, you are the moon, you are the fireflies. You are everything and everything is part of you. You have no more choices because choice has to do with separation and you are not separate. You are the universe. In this state, everything is appropriate and you *are* "the peace that passeth all understanding."

You begin by first being aware of the addiction you have to the behaviours that conceal your disturbance. Then, do not reinforce your behaviour. Do not reinforce your anger, your superiority, your inferiority. Do not give them any energy. It will all die away and you will come back to the root of your disturbance. Be with your disturbance. Allow it to be there, give it permission and suddenly you will see it all. You will see your disturbance and then you will realise there is a see–er. As you realise this level, all the levels become separate from you.

This is your possibility of gaining freedom. Freedom comes with disconnecting from your cover–up behaviour. It comes with disconnecting from the root of your disturbance and realising your essential self. This does not mean your behaviours will disappear completely, but, as you create distance between your behaviour and your essential self, everything else begins to fade away without effort. And as each behaviour falls away you are allowing your freedom. You are home, at last.

"The power of Yes can change existence.
The entire universe is affected when
someone says Yes from a very deep place."

Chapter XVIII

Living In the Vibration of Yes

The air is not empty. It is full and moving constantly. When you pass your hand through the air, the whole universe is affected because everything is a vibration. When someone enters a room and they are grumpy, you are affected by their presence. When they come in laughing, you are again affected. This occurs on visual and auditory levels and also on the level of energy and of vibrations. When I say vibrations, I am not referring to anything spiritual or esoteric, I am talking about something more scientific—wavelengths that can be detected and measured by sensitive instruments, such as radar, electron microscopy and kirlian photography.

Wherever you are, there are vibrations. The air is pulsing

with electromagnetic waves that radio stations and communications satellites hook into. If you brought a TV into the room where you are reading this and installed an aerial, you could pick up signals that are here now. The air is full of signals. In addition to those I have mentioned, there are many more levels of which you are even less aware. You affect them and they affect you.

All of the life experiences you have created for yourself have left a vibration in your system in the form of cellular memory. Everything is there, not only your experiences but the experiences of the whole universe. Everything is vibrating in you.

People often grow serious when they talk about waking up. As soon as we become serious we lower the frequency at which we vibrate. Seriousness closes us down and the more serious we become, the less likely we are to move into the expanded space of awakening. We cannot use our will to make ourselves happy or joyful but we can be aware when we are becoming serious and contracted—if, of course, we are ready not to take our seriousness so seriously.

The lower the rate at which we vibrate, the worse we feel. The higher we vibrate, the better we feel. We could say the higher the vibration, the closer to God, whatever that may mean to you. The practical thing is, when we vibrate at a higher frequency, we feel better. The natural state of our systems is to continually move towards a finer vibration. They will continue expanding on their own the more we move out of the way and allow it. Having fun, feeling the delight of life and feeling grateful expand us and raise our vibration. Fear lowers our vibration—fear of consequences, fear of how people see us, fear that they may like us or not like us, fear that we are doing the wrong thing. In fear we contract and are far less available to life.

Complaint also lowers our vibration. When we complain, we send out vibrations that come back to affect us and increase our discomfort. Our complaints generate what we will call a negative vibration, which is responded to by a negative vibration. When we put out joy, joy comes back.

In the New Testament it is said, "As you sow, so you will reap." One of our interpretations of what this means is that the way we are affects the way we are. The New Age has said that we create our own reality and we have developed some rather distorted ideas about the significance of that, often connected with self–blame. Yet the fact is we are always creating our own reality, moment to moment. Once you get in touch with the depth of this, it is breathtaking. It is so vast that you may go through stages where you do not want to move or say anything. You feel paralysed because anything you do or think impacts everything else and comes back to affect you.

There is nothing you can do about this, because of course, the more contracted you feel, the more you radiate a tense energy, then that energy boomerangs and everything worsens.

This is the basic key: There is nothing we can do; nothing at all. And that is difficult for us because we have been taught to "do." We have been told we can make it better, we can change it. We can do therapy to deal with it; we can go back to our childhood or past lives and we can fix it. None of that is true. We cannot fix anything; we cannot do anything. We are helpless. The only real option we have is to become more present and aware and accepting, in each moment.

This is it. It is very simple—the only thing there is to do is be choicelessly aware and allowing. If you are feeling uncomfortable, feel the discomfort, feel whatever is there. You have been trained to try to change it. You have been conditioned to think about it rather than be with it. None of this is working, neither for you, nor for the entire planet. Focusing on the outside never works in an ongoing way. Nothing in itself on the outside works— nothing. When you become more conscious, more aware and allowing, everything will simply change on its own.

The invitation now is to dare to stop doing and to start experiencing more fully whatever is there for you. When you are upset, feel upset; when you are afraid, be afraid; when you are in chaos, be in chaos and when you feel joy, feel the depth of your joy. That is the invitation—feel it and then share it responsibly.

Some of you may be thinking that you do not want to feel pain. Let us take a moment to consider that. Anything we resist is painful. Pain is resistance, it is contraction. It is the vibration of "no," of againstness. Any time we accept something, we will experience joy. Joy is acceptance, it emanates from the vibration of "yes." Comfort flows when we accept, discomfort comes when we reject. It is that simple. When we accept our disturbance totally it shifts and moves towards something else.

We have developed our neurosis from looking at life based on a fear that we might not survive. From this neurotic belief each of us is saying, "It has to be like this or I'm not going to be all right. I have to be treated in a certain way, seen in a certain way or I am going to be too uncomfortable." That is an attitude, not a fact. We are demanding conditions all the time: "Treat me this way and then I will be all right." But if you notice, you never do truly feel all right. When you operate out of this fear/demand, you are never deeply fulfilled inside.

When you demand that existence treat you in the way
you want to be treated, it is really your neurosis wanting its
way. It is not you. I am suggesting that you disconnect from
your neurosis and start to take responsibility for your
experience. What you feel is yours; no one else is to blame.
If you are feeling anger, that is your anger. Someone might
say something that offends you and the person sitting next
to you is not bothered at all by the comments. What is said
is not the source of your distress; your discomfort has to do
with you and not to do with others. When you really get the
depth of this, you will be living in a different universe—
your whole life will transform.

Your reactions have nothing to do with other people,
they are all about you. When you are not open, receptive
and allowing what you are feeling, you tend to react
unconsciously. Imagine someone has said something
derogatory about the opposite sex and you become angry
about it. That is about you, not about them; you have taken
something personally. Usually, if you get upset, what has been
said has some truth in it for you; you do not normally get
disturbed when it is completely untrue. Something will have
touched you—but you want to change the other person, you
want to change their opinion or their behaviour rather than
feel what is going on with you. You want to change them so
that you might feel better.

If you want real change to occur, you need to experience fully what you are feeling in each moment. Be present to what is happening. Do not try to change it, do not try to understand it. Do not work on it, do not do therapy with it. Simply feel what you feel, take responsibility for your experience and you will change. The place that has been stirred inside you will come into balance and complete itself when you allow it.

We are all helpless. There is nothing we can do. We are helpless—but it is not hopeless. It becomes hopeless when we attempt to change something and recognise how nothing we do really makes a difference. Yet all the time we are receiving help. We are helpless and there *is* help available, every single moment. Every thought we have, everything that happens in our lives, offers the possibility of support.

Your mind and the neurosis that originates there work in duality. They are constantly sorting out what is comfortable and what is not comfortable; what you will accept and what you will reject. Your neurosis keeps designing your life for you. The neurosis, however, does not know what you need, it only knows what it wants. It filters out anything it does not want and that is usually exactly what you need. If you get upset when someone says something, you usually need to hear that, because you are not clear or balanced in that area and the upset can alert you to this.

Take a look at how often you avoid life as it is. How often do you say, "I want it to be different"? When you do, you are demanding that life treat you differently and this demand creates your pain.

Let us imagine some examples. Your partner says they are attracted to someone else. Stage 2, they are going to spend time with that person. Stage 3, they are not coming back to you. Stage 4, they are telling you all the things they have withheld for the last seventeen years of living together. The feelings you are likely to have could be called pain and discomfort, but I am suggesting to you that they are resistance. You are not accepting what is and that creates your distress.

I invite you to take as an hypothesis that existence is always giving you what you need, in every moment, to support your expansion. Because we place conditions on life, we are not likely to experience all of these as opportunities to become more awake. We try to control others by broadcasting in various ways what people are allowed and not allowed to tell us. We are living nourishing, supportive existences that are moving us toward the areas in which we are not complete or in which we are out of balance—in order to set us free. And yet we keep resisting those situations. We persist in letting the neurosis choose what we think will make us comfortable, even though we do not ultimately feel fulfilled in our lives.

The alternative is to recognise that in any moment, this is what has come up for us; we can choose to be with it and be with what we are feeling about it. We cannot do anything or control anything. We can only respond to this moment. *Existence keeps giving us what we need.* All that is necessary is to be here totally and we will come into balance.

Most of us are looking for major breakthroughs. We are waiting for flashing lights and neon signs. It does not happen that way. The possibility of waking up, of coming into balance, of feeling fulfilled, is here in every moment. Whatever we think, whatever we feel, whatever we do, we are getting exactly what we need. When we make ourselves available to the moment, when we live in the vibration of "yes," each moment will move us toward freedom.

Living in the present, for most people, is not enough. It is not exciting enough; it is too empty; it is not sufficiently entertaining. Our senses have become dulled and we are no longer sensitive. When we look at a flower, we do not really see it. We do not hear the birds, we do not see the beauty. We have desensitized ourselves to such an extent that this moment seems boring. As we become more aware, we also become more sensitive and more alive and every moment becomes overflowingly full. It does not feel as necessary to go to the past, to demand our way or to use our will to make things happen. It does not feel necessary to seek or create excitement. We simply start to live each moment as it unfolds, even when it feels uncomfortable.

If you want to be a concert pianist there is a lot of hard work involved. You practise the scales and chords for hours and hours until you start to grow new channels in your brain that produce an entirely different sensitivity between your fingers and your central nervous system. Those hours of attention actually alter the topography of the brain. Perhaps you may complain about it, but if you want to be a concert pianist passionately, you really do want to practise. Your complaint has no basis, it is not real; it is just a game, a way of getting sympathy or attention. Deep down you know you are going to keep practising, because in your heart, you want to become a concert pianist.

If you want to wake up, you go through uncomfortable times, but all your complaints will have no depth because you want to wake up—even though you do not know what waking up is. Even though you have read about it, and heard about it, you do not really know what it is. Still, something in you knows that this is what you are here for.

If you want your maximum potential, it means being available all the time to something you do not really know about. It means that you are ready to go into each moment, however it presents itself to you, however uncomfortable it may be. And it does not have to be uncomfortable.

Everything is always for you, ready to take you to another level when you accept and say "yes" to the moment. Even if you do not accept it, existence is offering a reminder. It is giving you an opportunity to move into the flow of life and the maximum potential of each moment.

When you are in this flow and being total, there is a sense of deep satisfaction, moment–to–moment. If you think slightly ahead you have lost it. It is only available when you are here, present, now. It is in this flow that the maximum potential is realised. You do not have to worry about the meaning of existence or wonder if you are fulfilling your life. You do not have to think about anything at all. You are just here as totally as you know how to be.

It is an adventure and we are all on an incredible journey. If you want your adventure to be at your maximum potential, you need to look for trouble, not avoid it. Invite it. Most of us tend to do just the opposite. We play it safe and keep out of the way, to avoid certain people and uncomfortable situations. As we hold back in this way we create a great deal of tension and feel locked up inside. If you want to set yourself free, you have to put out an advertisement that says: I AM AVAILABLE.

We usually put out a sign that says KEEP AWAY and includes a threat of how we are going to hold others at a distance: I am going to get angry at you; I am going to become cynical; I am going to get hard, close off; I will withdraw my love; I will make you feel bad or feel guilty. We need to take a look at these behavioural patterns that say "go away." We have designed our lives to get people off our backs—our parents, our teachers, the authorities, and this keeps us locked into a place that is not balanced.

If you want your maximum potential, you need to take down the sign and make a declaration that you are making yourself available. And then go looking for trouble! When you allow an unconditional "yes" before the mind checks it out, you will vibrate differently. It is time to let yourself dance with the possibility of "yes" and allow life to come to you at another depth.

Chapter XIX
The Struggle Is Over

This final chapter can help you remember to be more gentle with yourself. The experience can be deepened if it is read to you while you close your eyes. Another possibility is to record it and then listen as your own voice offers this reminder.

Now take some time to be with what is going on. Open to all for which you feel grateful. Allow yourself to disconnect from the things about yourself you have not accepted. Let your heart open to all that you do appreciate about yourself, all that you enjoy, everything you love. Take a breath in, and as you do, feel that love, appreciation and gratitude go deep inside—bathing and nourishing every cell.

You have been hammering those cells with your complaints, your difficulties, your judgments. Recharge them now with your love, your caring and gratitude. As you breathe in, take in the air, and as you breathe out, let the energy flow through your whole body—to your fingertips, to your toes, to the top of your head. As you breathe out, imagine the breath and the energy dancing through all the cells, spinning them, throwing off the old and starting to vibrate with the new—cleaner, lighter, brighter.

Now listen to me very gently. The parts of you that you have not been loving are under great strain. The parts of your body that you do not like, the thoughts and behaviours you have not been accepting, the emotions you have not wanted to feel—you have been cursing them every time you have not wanted them. Imagine now, as you feel the love and the gratitude with each breath you take in and breathe out, that you are sending love and caring to those parts of you that need your support.

If you have not been accepting your anger, if you have been angry about your anger, that is cursing it. Instead, bless it, support it, care for it, so it can start to move. If there is a part of your body that you do not like, you have probably been cursing it without realising it. Because your body is not the shape or the weight you want, or because it has given you trouble or pain, you have gone against it and burdened it with your judgment. Instead now, love it and care for it. Take along your preference for how you would like it to be, but just lightly, as a preference, not as a demand. Do not put more pressure on that part of you. Take a moment to do the same with your automatic behaviours. Instead of being against them, take along your preference that you would like them to shift, but in a loving, caring and supportive way.

Planet Earth is a challenging place to be. It was designed that way—to be an adventurous training ground. When you do something that takes you out of balance, instead of blaming yourself for missing an opportunity or for going unconscious, bring in your love and your caring.

Let us take this a bit further now. There are people in your life that you have found it difficult to be with. It may seem that they have been against you or made your life hard. But take another look. They have been giving you opportunities. You may not have recognised it then, but look again now. The more unpleasant they have been, the bigger the opportunity for you to find that place of love and acceptance in yourself. It is comparatively easy to love the people who are supportive, but with people who are not, it is an opportunity for you to go deeper into your love. If you find there is someone you cannot love, who seems to be an enemy and impossible to love at the moment, do not blame yourself for not loving them. Do not stop the love for yourself because you are not loving them. Just remind yourself, "This is the way it is at the moment."

We are not denying what we usually call the heavy side, the dark side, the negative side. Instead of being against it, we are going *with* it. If you have cut your finger and it is painful, you do not hit it because you are upset at it. You clean it, put something on it, bind it up. You help it to heal. You take care of it.

Very gently, very quietly, see if you can allow this possibility inside. You are going to start your life again— now. Let go of all the things you have missed, the regrets, all the old ways you have been. You are going to begin with as much awareness, as much support and as much caring as you can bring, in each moment. Do not be against anything, not even your own againstness. Gently allow yourself to stay more in your heart, more in your caring for yourself and one another.

And remember—This Is It. This moment. Each Moment. Your life starts right now. In each moment, anything is possible. Anything.

Notes and References

Chapter I

Heraclitus (p. 2)
Greek philosopher; stressed importance of change and impermanence. He flourished in the Greek city of Ephesus, on the Ionian coast of what is now Turkey, at the end of the sixth century B.C.

Lao Tzu (p. 2)
(also Lao-tse, Lao-tsze) 604–531 B.C. approximately. Chinese philosopher; founder of Taoism; wrote *Tao Te Ching*. This book has been translated more frequently than any work except the Bible. His philosophy is simple: Accept what is in front of you without wanting the situation to be other than it is. Study the natural order of things and work with it rather than against it, for to try to change what is only sets up resistance.

Jesus Christ (p. 2)
"But rather seek ye first the kingdom of God; and all these things shall be added to you."   Matthew 6:33, New Testament

"And the peace of God, which passeth all understanding, shall keep [guard] your hearts and minds through Christ Jesus."
Philippians 4:7, New Testament

Buddha (p. 3)
Born Siddhartha Gautama into royalty in the sixth century B.C. in what today is Nepal. Realising that worldly comforts did not ensure happiness and moved by the suffering he saw around him, he abandoned his position, wealth and family to seek the truth. After years of study and meditation as an ascetic monk, Gautama experienced enlightenment, he realised the cause of all human suffering and how it could be overcome. From that moment onward, his followers called him Buddha and he spent the rest of his life teaching. He died at the age of eighty. Many different schools of Buddhism have evolved from his original teachings.

Buddha speaks of his experience in a discourse called "What the Teaching Is Not. The Supreme Net." From the *Brahmajala Sutta*

Chapter II

Jesus Christ (p. 20)
"When you make the two one, and when you make the inner as the outer and the outer as the inner and the above as the below, and when you make the male and the female into a single one, so that the male will not be male and the female [not] be female, when you make eyes in the place of an eye, and a hand in the place of a hand, and a foot in the place of a foot, [and] an image in the place of an image, then shall you enter [the kingdom]." Log. 22, 85:24

"The Gospel According to Thomas," Coptic text translated by A. Guillaumont, H.-Ch. Puech, G. Quispel, W. Till.

Chapter IV

"Thou art That." (p. 31)
Phrase from Hindu text, Upanishad. "He is the Supreme Brahman, the Self of all, the chief foundation of this world, subtler than the subtle, eternal. That thou art; Thou art That."
Atharva Veda, Kaivalya Upanishad 16

The Upanishads were composed about 600 B.C.; they are mystical-philosophical meditations on the meaning of existence and the nature of the universe and form the basis of Hinduism.

Hinduism
The most prevalent religion of India, based on the religion of the original Aryan settlers as expounded and evolved in the Vedas, the Upanishads and the Bhagavad-Gita. Hinduism is extremely diversified with many schools of philosophy and theology, popular cults, and a pantheon symbolising many various attributes of a single god. Statistically, there are over 700 million Hindus, mainly in India and Nepal. Hinduism is not strictly a religion; it is based on the practice of Dharma, the code of life. It is considered one of the oldest religions.

Om (p. 31)
Om is one of the most sacred words and symbols depicted in the Upanishads, the ancient Hindu scriptures. It stands for the Total or Ultimate Reality, which is at once personal and impersonal, immanent and transcendent. As such it is a symbol of Brahman (God) in its immanent aspect. Om is the unity of all sounds, and all matter and energy are reduced to it.

Chapter V

"Koan" (p. 35)
An impossible riddle such as: "What were the colour of your eyes before you were conceived?" A person has to think on it until their mind gives up and thinks nothing. In that moment, when the mind stops, without thinking on yesterday or tomorrow and being totally in the present, there is a gap—this is "satori." This method comes from Zen Buddhist traditions.

"Satori" (p. 36)
Enlightenment is called "satori" in Japan and it is obtained by means of "koans" and "zazen" (sitting meditation) with the help of a Master (roshi). This may take years or can happen in an instant. Satori is an uncommon, but normal experience. Awareness of one's self as an individual temporarily disappears and there follows a spontaneous blossoming of awareness of the real nature of creation.

Jesus Christ (p. 36)
"But rather seek ye first the kingdom of God; and all these things shall be added to you."   Matthew 6:33, New Testament

Chapter VII

Jesus Christ (p. 48)
"Take therefore no thought for the morrow: for the morrow shall take thought for the things of itself."   Matthew 6:34, New Testament

(p. 48)
"Consider the lilies of the field, how they grow; they toil not, neither do they spin: and yet I say unto you, that even Solomon in all his glory was not arrayed like one of these."   Matthew 6:28, New Testament

(p. 51)
"Unless you become like a little child you can not enter the kingdom of God."   Matthew 18:3, New Testament

Chapter VIII

Karma (p. 58)
This has many meanings in Hinduism. It means actions one does as well as the effect of actions and past actions. Karma is divided into four categories: sanchita karma, or the accumulated past actions; prarabdha karma, or that part of sanchita karma which results in this present birth and is known as predestination; kriyamana karma, or present willful actions, or free will; and agami karma, or the immediate results caused by our present actions.   Sant Keshavedas, 8

Sins of the father . . . (p. 58)
" . . .Visiting the iniquity of fathers on the children and on the grandchildren to the third and fourth generations."
                          Exodus 34:7, Old Testament

Chapter XII

Socrates (p. 90)
(c. 469–399 B.C.) Born in Athens, rejected the popular conceptions of

the Greek gods and their relation to humans. He believed that divine providence had to do with the creation of the world; that man's body was a dwelling place of the soul and what happened to the soul was more important than what happened to the body. He was accused of being a menace to society by officials whom he had criticised. They accused him of corrupting the minds of the young and rejecting the gods of Athens. At his trial, Socrates defended himself and his manner of living and presented sufficient evidence to show that the accusations brought against him were without foundations. However, the jury voted against him. He was sentenced to death by the poisonous plant extract, hemlock.

Mother Shipton (p. 90)
Lived in fifteenth century England and predicted important historical events many years ahead of time: the defeat of the Spanish Armada in 1588, the Great Fire of London in 1666, the advent of modern technology. She wrote her prophecies in the form of poems. Today her predictions are still proving uncannily accurate.

Edgar Cayce (p. 90)
Between the years 1901 and 1945, Edgar Cayce, called "The Sleeping Prophet," gave over 14,000 psychic readings including accurate medical diagnosis and treatments, information on prehistoric civilizations including Atlantis and many correct predictions.

Mayans (p. 90)
A book called the *Dresden Codex*, named after the German city in whose library it was lodged, was brought from what is now Central America. It was inscribed with unknown hieroglyphs, written by Maya Indians who once ruled over much of Central America. In 1880 a German scholar cracked the code of the Mayan calendar, making it possible for other scholars to translate the many dated inscriptions to be found on buildings, stelae and other ancient Mayan artifacts. The content, concerned with astronomy, provided detailed tables of lunar eclipses and other phenomena. These were so accurate that they put our own calendar to shame. From their start date this Mayan Prophecy points to a date in our own time, 22 December 2012, as the end of the world.

Bankei (p. 92)
Zen Master living in the late seventeenth century in Japan.

"We are not born, we will not die. . . ."
"There can be no death for what was never born, so if it is unborn, it is obviously undying. The Unborn is the origin of all and the beginning of all. There is no source born. So being unborn means dwelling at the very source of all Buddhas." From the Ryumon-Ji Sermon

Jesus Christ (p. 96)
"If you continue in my word you are truly my disciples and you will know the truth and the truth will make you free."
John 8:32, New Testament

Chapter XV

George Gurdjieff (p.117)
Born Georgii Gurdzhiev in the late nineteenth century in Russia. In 1922, he founded the Institute for the Harmonious Development of Man in France. He studied medicine and the priesthood, but left everything to search for ultimate answers. From 1894 to 1912, he travelled in Asia and the Middle East seeking esoteric wisdom. He was influenced by Sufism and blended this with other spiritual teachings. He believed his ideas needed to be rediscovered by his students and stimulated this discovery with strenuous activities similar to that of Marpa, thirteenth-century Tibetan teacher of Milarepa. Gurdjieff's writings include *All and Everything* and *Meetings With Remarkable Men*.

U. G. Krishnamurti (p. 118)
Contemporary philosopher from India, currently living in Switzerland. He has been called a "spiritual terrorist." He overturns all accepted beliefs on God, mind, soul, enlightenment, religion, humanity, heart, love, relationships. He doesn't offer hope, love, peace or spiritual salvation. He discourages people from coming to see him and most often politely turns them away.

John Wren-Lewis (p. 118)
He is an awakened man who is unusual because, in spite of having many strong opinions based on a lifetime of intelligent and scientific exploration, he remains open-minded and ever-curious. Prior to his experience of awakening, he published extensively and held several professorial appointments in the United States and the United Kingdom

as a mathematical physicist and humanistic psychologist. He is currently finishing *The 9:15 to Nirvana*, a book that further elaborates on the subject of his awakening. He lives outside Sydney, Australia, with his wife, the author Ann Faraday.

"When I'm tired I sleep, when I'm hungry, I eat. . . ." (p. 123)
Bankei, Zen Master living in the late seventeenth century in Japan. He opened a Zen school not far away from another Buddhist teacher. Many students from the first school began to attend Bankei's lectures. The other school's Master called on Bankei, who was in the middle of a lecture. The first Master scolded his students for abandoning his school, and yelled at Bankei, saying that *his* teacher could perform miracles such as walking on water and signing his name from the other side of a river. Bankei replied, "My miracle is that when I'm hungry, I eat, and when I am tired, I sleep."

Chapter XVII
Jesus Christ (p. 140)
"Verily, verily I say unto you except a man be born again, he can not see the kingdom of God." John 3:3, New Testament

Chapter XVIII
Jesus Christ (p.143)
"For whatever a man soweth, that shall he also reap."
Galatians 6:7, New Testament

All Bible quotes have been taken from the King James Version, American Bible Society.

In Each Moment

Acknowledgments

During the years 1995 through 1998 I was part of a group of people who travelled with Ava and Paul Lowe. We lived and worked together, supporting the gatherings all over the world where we met and Paul spoke. Many of these people contributed to the creation of this project.

Although the book itself only began to be a reality in the last fifteen months of that time, it originates in the longing many of us have had for something more in life and the courage we drew on to leave behind our familiar worlds and move into the unknown, to experiment with living in a new way and to give something back. It has been, and continues to be, a great adventure. There are a few people I would like to acknowledge for the special joy we have shared in creating this book and for the companionship of the journey we are taking together.

Thank you Kira Kay, for the countless hours you have devoted to taping Paul's talks. Thanks also to Treasure Miller and Sabine Geiger for the creative proofreading, excellent suggestions, encouragement and laughter; Shana Lowe for your uncompromising assistance in editing; Penny Berton for inspiration for the title; Louise Bélisle for your enduring friendship and stepping so totally into the gap that left me free to devote my time to this project; Dov Glock for your loving and abiding faith in my ability and in me; Ava Lowe for the support, honesty and refusal to let me be less than I am and the encouragement to be more than I imagined.

And Paul Lowe, thank you for the inspiration of your words and your being, for your devotion to the truth, your total availability and willingness to lovingly shake us up so that we may discover a new depth of ourselves. And thank you for the continual reminder not to take anything too seriously.

Devon Ronner

Ava & Paul Lowe

We hope you have enjoyed this book. If you would like to spend time with Ava & Paul as they travel around the world offering talks, weekend and two- and three-week gatherings, you may obtain an international schedule of their events by sending in the Order Form on the following pages.

"We help you to see how you are not living life your way and assist you to dare to live your own uniqueness; to set yourself free. When you are truly being yourself, the world is nourished."   Ava & Paul Lowe

Other Works Available by
Paul Lowe

IN EACH MOMENT
ALSO AVAILABLE AT YOUR LOCAL BOOKSTORE

FOR ORDERS IN THE UNITED STATES
PAID IN U.S. FUNDS

___ copies In Each Moment @ $14.95 $_____
___ copies The Experiment Is Over @ $14.95 $_____
___ copies CD Sound and Silence @ $14.95 $_____
Shipping & Handling charges for 1st item $ 3.50
Add $2 for each additional item $_____
In California, add 7.5% sales tax $_____
Total enclosed $_____

Please send a Catalogue of Audio & Video Tapes   _____
Please send Ava & Paul Lowe's
   Schedule of Worldwide Events   _____

Name _____

Address _____

City _____ State _____

Zip Code _____ Country _____

Phone _____ Fax _____

e-mail _____ Date _____

Please make your check or money order payable to: S. Ronner
Enclose your payment with this form and mail to: S. Ronner
1413 Argyle, Montreal, QC H3G 1V5, Canada
Fax: 1 (514) 939-0382
e-mail: ineachmoment@sprynet.com
http:// www.ineachmoment.com

Thank you for your order

ORDER FORM
IN EACH MOMENT
ALSO AVAILABLE AT YOUR LOCAL BOOKSTORE

FOR ORDERS IN CANADA
PAID IN CANADIAN FUNDS

___ copies In Each Moment @ $19.95 $_____
___ copies The Experiment Is Over @ $19.95 $_____
___ copies CD Sound and Silence @ $19.95 $_____

Shipping & Handling charges for 1st item $ 5.00
Add $3 for each additional item $_____
Total enclosed $_____

Please send a Catalogue of Audio & Video Tapes   _____
Please send Ava & Paul Lowe's
    Schedule of Worldwide Events   _____

Name _____

Address _____

City _____ Province _____

Postal Code _____ Country _____

Phone _____ Fax _____

e-mail _____ Date _____

Please make your cheque or money order payable to: S. Ronner
Enclose your payment with this form and mail to: S. Ronner
1413 Argyle, Montreal, QC H3G 1V5 Canada
Fax: 1 (514) 939-0382
e-mail: ineachmoment@sprynet.com
http:// www.ineachmoment.com

Thank you for your order